# PLAIN AND HAPPY LIVING

———————

*Amish Recipes And Remedies*

*By Emma Byler*
*(Jonas Em)*

Goosefoot Acres Press
CLEVELAND, OHIO

ISBN 1-879863-71-5

Cover design:  Robert Tubbesing

Illustrations by:  Mallie Kimbrell

Published by:

 Goosefoot Acres Press
Division of Goosefoot Acres, Inc.
P.O. Box 18016
Cleveland, OH 44118-0016
(216) 932-2145

**Library of Congress Cataloging-in-Publication Data**

Byler, Emma, 1921–
    Plain and happy living : Amish recipes and remedies / by Emma Byler (Jonas Em).
        p.   cm.
    Includes index.
    ISBN 1-879863-70-7 : $9.95.
    ISBN 1-879863-71-5 : $9.95.
    1. Cookery, Amish.   2. Amish—Ohio—Social life and customs. 3. Folk medicine—Ohio—Formulae, receipts, prescriptions.
    I. Title
    TX715.B9882   1992
    640'.41'088287—dc20                                  92–6121
                                                          CIP

9 7 5        4 6 8

# FOREWORD

It's not until you get to know the Amish that you realize how much we have lost of what was once common knowledge and practice in society as a whole. In effect, the Amish community is in many ways a living museum of the values, knowledge, skills, and practices which were common as recently as forty or fifty years ago but which have been subtly and progressively lost as technology and specialization have pervaded our lives.

One of the major lessons we can learn from the Amish is how to use natural plant materials for healing. The Amish believe that God put all that man needs in plants and that our job is to learn to use them as He intended for both food and medicine.

In discussing the relative merits of natural versus synthetic medicines, Dr. James Duke, economic botanist with the U.S. Department of Agriculture, said:

> *"Most herbs...contain vitamins, minerals, fibers, antioxidants, antitumor agents and antiseptics, and many if not all, contain in addition several other types of bioactive compounds. Leaves of herbs are particularly rich in vitamins A, C, and E, iron, calcium and fibers.... [If the right ones are taken regularly, the] human body is pretty good at grabbing from [them] those things it needs."*

As we "Yankees" move back to natural remedies, we would be wise to draw from the respository of herbal knowledge and experience found in the Amish and other cultural groups still practicing the old ways.

The Amish are descendants of the Swiss Anabaptist movement of the 1520's, started by a group of young Catholic monks who separated themselves from the 16th century church in Switzerland to live according to Christ's example — plainly, simply, without ritual, and committed to sacrificing for one another. Their lifestyle is based on old, labor-intensive practices and emphasizes spiritual over material values. They live very much like their (and our) ancestors did in the 19th and early 20th centuries. Those who are exemplary of the faith largely grow their own food, stay out of debt, build their own homes, and maintain neat, attractive farms and homes with gardens and lots of flowers. They walk or drive buggies, use relatively little fossil fuel, and raise very large families (eight to ten children are common). Farming, followed by lumber production and woodworking in all its forms are their primary occupations. Because of their frugality and self-sufficiency, they are in many ways insulated from the crises which so often disrupt modern society.

Each community has its practitioners of natural medicine. Since the Amish believe that education beyond the eighth grade is unnecessary for their lifestyle and exposes their children to too much worldly knowledge, none are college trained. They pick up their skills from others on the job, supplemented in some cases by correspondence courses and extensive reading.

The Geauga County, Ohio, Amish community is no exception. Its folk medicine practitioners range from those selling commercially-prepared herbal formulas and naturopath/reflexologists trained through correspondence to those few whose knowledge of folk medicine has been handed down to them through the generations.

Emma A. Byler is one of the latter.

Emma is a vibrant, healthy 70-year-old widow of 36 years. She has ten children, all of whom are grown and providing her with multitudes of grandchildren. She weaves rugs, makes quilts, gardens, cans food, and travels considerably to visit relatives. Age hasn't slowed her down a bit. Emma treats most of her ills with herbal remedies passed down from her father, who learned them from an old Indian from Kansas who lived in Northeastern Ohio for a time in the early 1900's.

She gathers some of the plants she needs from the wild each year and grows most of the rest. She has available a ready remedy for just about anything that ails her and her family. Home remedies for common, and sometimes even uncommon, ills are particularly important when there is little or no money to pay a doctor.

In her lifetime, Emma has collected a wealth of insights, ideas, remedies, and tips for happy living. It is a pleasure to introduce her to you, so that you can learn at her feet as I have.

Peter Gail, Ph.D., Director
Goosefoot Acres Center for Wild Vegetable Research and Education
Windsor, OH 44099
May, 1991

I dedicate this book to my mother,

**AMANDA MILLER BYLER HOCHSTETLER**

**Born March 6, 1900 and 91 years young as this is written.**

Without our kind and caring mother, the life of us twelve children would have been bleak and dreary indeed. My mother taught us good from evil with kind words and deeds.

We also had a kind and loving father, but he had a little stronger method of teaching us the truth. So this combination of our bringing up worked out very well.

My mother is in good health and uses no medication of any kind except maybe an aspirin now and then. She feels it is a waste of time to see a doctor, and the word "cane" is an insult to her.

# ACKNOWLEDGEMENTS

Thank you, Peter Gail.

I cannot with truth say, "I wrote this book." But I do selfishly call it "my book." The notes of ideas, recipes, and things remembered in my growing up years were all faithfully gathered into a pile. My father was uppermost in my mind during this time. He had hereditary heart disease and was deathly afraid of drugs and hospitals, and so he studied and gathered and dried the God-given medicine that grew around us until even doctors became interested.

As I was getting older, the realization began to dawn on me that if a book of what I had learned from him and others was going to be published to preserve this heritage, someone else would have to do it.

Two summers ago I met Peter Gail for the first time. He was very interested in these notes and bits and pieces I had written down, and offered to take them and make some semblance of a draft for me. After much editing, culling, and tossing, this book is the result.

And so, my friends, I hope it will bring you a few bright moments.

Emma Byler
(Jonas Em)
Middlefield, OH
May, 1991

# A NOTE FROM THE PUBLISHER

This is the first of a number of books to be written by Amish and non-Amish authors about the Amish for Goosefoot Acres Press.

An objective of this and forthcoming books is to share valuable information with all our readers in order to preserve and interpret the Amish culture as a model of simplified living which emphasizes love, service, and sacrifice -- a life which, if lived in its ideal, will lead to joy, contentment, and fulfillment.

Non-Amish readers may find the book more interesting after a couple of the Amish practices and colloquialisms are explained.

- The Amish generally refer to non-Amish as either "Yankees" or "English", depending on which settlement you are in. When the Amish began immigrating to the Pennsylvania colony in the early 1700's, they settled among "English" (loyal to the English monarchy) and "Yankees" (anxious to form their own country) settlers. After the Yankees prevailed in the Revolutionary War, other groups seeking new lifestyles and freedom from persecution began pouring in from all over the world. The Amish saw little need to distinguish between the various ethnic groups of Germans, Norwegians, Poles, or the like, and conveniently applied the terms "Yankees" or

"English" to anyone not a member of their unique community.

- Because so many Amish have the same sur- and given names, they have developed several means to positively identify one another.

  One way is to establish nicknames for individuals and couples. The most common is to combine the husband's and wife's names to form the nickname. Emma Byler, married as she was to Jonas Byler, is known in their community as "Jonas Em." You will notice our use of her nickname on the title page.

If you find other uses in the book which are not clear to you, please call them to our attention. We will include an explanation in subsequent printings.

# CONTENTS

# DISCLAIMER

The herbal folk remedies contained in this book are included for information only. Neither Emma Byler nor Peter Gail are medical doctors, and do not presume to prescribe. If you choose to use any of these remedies, you do so at your own risk.

Every person's body is different and responds differently to particular plant products. Allergic reactions may result from use of the natural remedies suggested in this book. If you know, or suspect, that you have food-related or other allergies, consult with your physician **before** using the products introduced to you in this book. It is also very important that you consult with your doctor when ill and follow his/her recommendations.

## De Alt Frau im Shoo

*Is var un alta frau*
*See hut gvonned in a shoo*
*See hut so feel kinna cot*
*See vayst net vas zu do*

*See gebt se som brote*
*Un a glay shtickly speck*
*Un pattled see hot*
*Un shicked see ins bet.*

## Un Glenna Grumma Man

*Is vor un glenna grumma*
*man*
*Er lauft un grumma mile*
*Un fint un grumma cent*
*Uff un glenna grumma pile*

*Er kauft un grumma katz*
*See funkt un glay grum micely*
*See vonna all zumma*
*In a glay grum hicely*

## The Old Woman in a Shoe

*There was an old woman*
*Who lived in a shoe*
*She had so many children*
*She didn't know what to do*

*She gave them some broth*
*And a little piece of bread*
*Spanked them all soundly*
*And sent them to bed.*

## A Little Crooked Man

*There was a little crooked*
*man*
*He walked a crooked mile*
*Found a crooked sixpence*
*Upon a crooked stile*

*He bought a crooked cat*
*She caught a crooked mouse*
*And they all lived together*
*In a little crooked house*

Two common nursery rhymes, in "Pennsylvania Dietch" dialect, with English translations.

# INTRODUCTION

This book is written as a folk lore so that this new generation can get a glimpse of our lives as they were in the days of yore -- let's say since 1900, the year my mother was born.

Mother can remember when the first cars came clattering down what is now State Route 87 in Middlefield, Ohio which was then still a dirt road.

Doctors of that time, who made their visits in horse and buggy, did not have medicines like we have today to combat diseases. When Father and Mother set their wedding date early in December, 1918, the flu broke out. Their wedding date came and passed because no one was able to come to the wedding as the neighbors were all sick. Many families lost one or two members and when there was a death, the dead would be buried and the funeral ceremony preached later when people were again able to go to church, weddings, and other events. I believe it was against the law to hold a gathering of any kind during this epidemic. I remember mother saying that quinine and bitters were given, and the doctor ordered everyone scattered throughout the house with as much fresh air as possible in each room. It seemed that those going outside to do chores regularly, if they came down with the flu at all, were the last to get it.

During the Depression, there was no money for doctors or medicine. When I was about ten years old (1932), an old Indian came from the West and moved into a tumbled-down shack up the road from our place. His cooking utensils were old and battered ones he had found on a junk pile. He came often to our place for milk and water and would show Dad the herbs, roots, and other materials he had gathered that day. He carried a large bag over his shoulder with a wide strap, and put everything he found in that bag. Once, he gave me a gold lock and a key. I was so proud of it that I carried it in a metal aspirin tin along with a nickel and several teeth I had lost a while before. I had a string pinched in the box as a handle and would swing this around. One time it slipped out of my hand and was lost forever. I now feel it probably flew up in the tree I was standing under and stayed there, which made my raking and cleaning of the grass and ground under the tree quite futile.

The Indian would gather his roots in the fall of the year after the seed buds were ripe and would carefully seed a new bed as he gathered, thus leaving a new crop for the future. In later years, my father found many of these beds and would then do the same. My nephew, Danny D. Miller, (another Geauga County Amish herbalist) is now finding some of these beds and harvesting the roots. This was primarily golden seal and ginseng, both of which are rather hard to find now.

From the time I was ten years old, being the oldest, I would tag along with my dad and help him hunt and gather. I learned much just by being with him and observing him. After I married at nineteen, I used these things with my family, because we still didn't have doctors who could come easily, and even if there had been, we didn't have money to pay them.

Not having money also meant that we couldn't just go to the store and buy things we wanted for the house or barn. So we had to make do with what we had around us, not only for medicine, but also for gardening, housekeeping, caring for our animals, making the house fresh, and even for coloring Easter eggs! I now pass these things along to you who read this to use if you want.

Mallie Kimbrell

# PART 1 -

# HUMBLE BEGINNINGS

*The road of life seems long*
*As we travel through the years*
*And with a heart that's broken*
*And eyes brimful of tears.*

*We falter in our weariness*
*And sink beside the way*
*But God leans down and whispers,*
*"Child, there'll be another day.*

*And the road will grow much smoother*
*And much easier to face*
*So do not be disheartened*
*This is just a resting place."*

*Author Unknown*

# CHAPTER 1 -

# GROWING UP AMISH DURING THE GREAT DEPRESSION

It seems today with so much convenience, people don't understand what is possible for them to do when they have to and what life was like for just about everyone not too many years ago.

The kind of winter we are having as I write this puts me in mind of some we had in the thirties, when I was from ten to twelve years old. We were poor and lived in an old farm house that never knew what insulation was. When it went down to zero or lower, we lived in the bedroom and living room altogether, had a stove in each room, and could not keep very warm at that. My father, "Yosta Jeckie," was oft times not well but managed to keep us in fuel and food, and we were never happier than when he was in the house making things. He would look at something and then could make it without a pattern--toys, baskets, ferneries, etc. He learned to make baskets from the Gypsies who traveled around Geauga County in covered wagons dealing in horses. During the winter, if he was lucky enough to get a green black ash log, he would keep it in the basement so that it wouldn't dry out. Then some morning we would hear the "bong, bong, bong" of the axe and he would be pounding a thin strip along the log to loosen the grain. Usually three or four strips would loosen with one pounding. He would bring up only what could be used in one day. These grains would have to all be trimmed to one width. Then the standards were scraped smooth and the strips to be woven were split (a trick not every basket weaver knows how to do). He made covered clothes hampers, wash baskets, shopping baskets, and egg baskets as well as some fancier ones to give as gifts to his family and friends. I have one he made for my eighth birthday, and it is now over sixty years old. He was always whistling this certain little tune while he worked, and if it changed at all, we all knew enough to move back well out of the way as evidently something had gone wrong!

He would buy a poisonous dye by the name of Aniline. He would dye some strips for borders--blue, green, and red. When the weather warmed up enough, he would hitch old Barney. (Anyone knowing my father would know the horse had to be old before he would drive him!) Anyway, he would load up the baskets and go off to peddle them. He usually set out for "Money Ridge" as that was where the money was in those days. At least us children grew up with that idea. Our relatives on Dad's side lived there, and they would send along a lot of goodies--hand-me-downs and things we would otherwise have done without.

Some days he would whittle. He made miniature rolling pins, potato mashers, games such as "Pick-Up-Sticks" (I still have a set of these), and also a wooden jumping jack that danced on a platform. When he was occupied at this task, he would have an audience of us children watching spellbound as he whittled and sang.

My growing up years were mostly happy ones. I would meet up with the neighbor children, maybe one-fourth mile from home as we lived the farthest east, and we always had a good time going to and coming home from school, walking the little more than two miles through sunshine, rain, and snow. In season, we ate anything eatable that grew along the way. I especially remember the old wild apple tree across the road from the Kivinemises (a Finnish family). We ate the apples until none were left, starting when they were still quite green.

The very first place I remember living was the farm at the top of Mespo Hill. It was at this place where I would get "spells" and Mom would give me "zunly druppa" (medicine for bad temper!).

I remember one day my dear mother was picking cherries when I had one of these spells. I hurt my arm flinging it around trying to get her attention and wouldn't use it the rest of the day. Dr. Clapp was called and found nothing at all wrong with my arm. Mother paid him with cherries she had picked.

After these spells, Mother would bundle me up and send me to the barn where Dad was doing chores. This happened quite often, and I learned to milk "ol' Jers" before I started school--in fact, I was just three years old. I think I must have been able to milk before I was properly house trained, because at that time my grandmother gave me a little cup and saucer with the verse "Little Jack Horner" on it to entice me to use the bathroom. I still have the cup today.

From the hill farm, we moved to the Gilson Farm, a place that had only an old granary for a house. We fixed it up with tar paper and stuffed rags in the cracks to keep out the cold wind. It was here that I learned about ghosts and ghoulies and things that went bump in the night. Mother would explain these noises away by saying it was only the wind whistling through the cracks. The living room ceiling was reddish resin paper tacked over the studs, and in the evening we could hear the patter and skirmishes of the mice running along on this paper. If it got too bad, Dad would wait until he could hear them coming and poke a stove poker up through the paper to see if he could kill one, which was something only a child would remember.

My Uncle Dan lived with us at the Gilson place, and he would help us get dressed and washed for the breakfast table. We could do this ourselves, but if we were slow, he would stand us on a chair, dip his hand in cold water, and swipe it across our faces, then wipe it with a towel. A couple of treatments like that, and we learned to wash ourselves very quickly.

We would get even with Uncle Dan by cracking hickory nuts and walnuts in front of his bed upstairs and not clean it up, so when he went to bed (usually in the dark), he would step on these sharp shells with his bare feet. Did we ruin the floor? No, this was a granary type of house and had rough planks for a floor!

From Gilson's, we went to the Difford Farm on Girdle Road. An old, old house, built on big stones rather than a foundation, stood behind the big house. It was tiny, but had a nice buttery with all handmade cupboard doors and shelves. It would be worth a lot of money today.

The house must have been about twenty-four feet square. It had a kitchen, but the bedroom and living room must have been all in one. We had our playhouse in there in summer. It was so muddy when we moved here in the spring that Pap Doddy's (Grandpa's) wagon almost tipped over and our straw tick fell off in the mud.

The Difford house was so cold in winter that we wore our coats and sometimes our overcaps (the heavy caps we wear outside) to bed upstairs. Insulation was still not made in those days, and the house didn't even have sheathing boards, just overlap siding and a lot of that was loose and curled. On the inside was plaster and lath and many coats of wallpaper. The area behind the bed where the heat wouldn't reach was always white with frost during a very cold spell. The living room floor had such wide cracks we didn't need a lamp when we went into the cellar in the evening. This house was of "salt box design" but had seen better days. It had high ceilings of 10' 2" but the roof sank in the middle, making it about 1 1/2 to 2 feet lower in the center of the roof than at the eaves. The rainwater collection pipe went down through the center of the house into a cistern in the basement. The roof was changed in later years, as it was very hard to keep it from leaking.

The day my Aunt Lydia married we went to the wedding in a one-horse bobsled. It was zero degrees that morning. We all bundled up in blankets and quilts and sat on a bed of straw. Dad ran along beside the sled to keep warm. By evening, it was storming--a white blizzard and still zero degrees or colder--so we stayed at Grandpa's and Dad went home alone.

When he got into the house, the fire was out and it was zero in the living room. He built up the fire and slept on the couch with his overcoat and boots on. He waited until afternoon when the storm had abated before he came to bring us home.

From the Difford place we moved to the Burr Gates Farm. It was here that brother Jake was added to the fold. It was so very cold that morning (32° below zero) that Dad didn't want to go after a hired girl, but it so happened that we were out of bread. My sister Lizzie and I were about nine and ten years old, so Mom, from her bed, told us how to stir up a batch of bread which made seven loaves. We got along real well until the bread was ready for the oven. We could only put in five loaves, so we set the other two loaves aside. Our kitchen range was so old and rickety that we had to fire it up as hot as we could until the bread was brown on top, then turn the loaves upside down and bake the bottom too. Well, so far so good, but it took so long to bake those first five loaves that after we put the last two loaves in the oven, we forgot all about the bread until the next day when someone happened to open the oven door. Lo and behold! There were the two loaves, hard as a rock. Now what should we do? Food and money were scarce, and we couldn't afford to waste either, so we didn't want to show the disaster to Mother. We stuck the two loaves into an empty flour bag and threw it into an old silo pit we were filling up with trash. But that was not the end of it! Several days later, I looked out the window and there was one of Dad's hound dogs sharpening his teeth on a white object that could be nothing else but the hard, dried-out bread we had thrown away. So out I went and smashed the loaf to dust with a hammer and scattered it to the four winds. It was not until many years later that Mother learned about the incident.

From the Burr Gates farm we moved to the place on the river. It was owned by an old man named Emery Easton. As I grew up, being the oldest, I worked outside with my dad a lot, Mother having several younger girls to help her. I was allowed to have a trap line in the swamp and along the river and could keep any of the money I made if I skinned the catch. This was usually muskrat, and boy, do they smell! I would plug my nose with cotton and get busy as three or four muskrats a week at $1.80 per pelt was nothing to sneeze at (not with a nose full of cotton, anyway!). I spent the money with care. In those days, I could buy a pair of shoes from the Alden's catalog for $1.98 and there was a popular dress goods (cotton type) that I could buy for eight cents a yard. I remember I had three good dresses once, not counting my black one.

One day Dad and I tracked a mink under a brush pile. The pile had only one entrance because the flood waters had frozen and then receded, encasing the whole pile in ice. So with me hanging on to "ol' Trailer" and Dad stomping on the brush pile, we soon had a nice mink. Because I was such a help and let go of the dog at the right time, Dad gave me a dollar. That night at the supper table, I found a handful of hickory nuts on my plate. This was my jealous sisters' way of telling me that they thought I was my dad's pet squirrel!

We lived on a farm of 100 acres, but could not afford to run it as such. There was no money for seed or fertilizer, so we raised only enough to feed ourselves, our one cow, and several horses. The horses were used for transportation and as beasts of burden in the field. We always had two pigs to butcher in the fall. These were our garbage disposals! Potato, apple and other parings, sweet corn cobs and stalks, pea pods, and any other kitchen refuse was always saved for the pigs. Even the dishes were rinsed before washing, and this gravy put in the swill pail for the hogs. The dish water containing homemade soap made of lye also ended up in the swill pail, as it was supposed to get rid of round worms the pigs had at times.

We picked wild blackberries and raspberries to can, and if we had more than we could use, we would peddle them in our small town for ten cents a quart. Mom canned green beans, peas, shell beans, beets, tomatoes, berries, and applesauce. Potatoes were stored in a slotted bin. Squash and pumpkins were stored where it was cool and dry and would keep until New Years. Cabbage heads were wrapped in newspaper and stored in the cool, dirt-floored basement. Mother would cook apple butter out in the yard in a big kettle. If we could afford sugar, well and good, but if we couldn't, maple syrup and other sweeteners were used. Milk and butter were no problem, having a cow to furnish these items.

My father would fix fences and keep the building in good repair to pay for the rent. He made our toys for Christmas. These included jumping jacks, small baskets, carved potato mashers, and rolling pins all made out of wood. Mom made dolls and doll carry-alls and new clothes for the ones we already had. Believe me, I never knew the words "Fisher Price" until I was a grandma to a dozen youngsters!

In my growing up years, our family never had much cash money, but our heritage is worth more than silver or gold, and we were happy. I never remember going hungry, and the clothes we had were good enough for us when we were at home, but when we had to go away among people and see the stares of other children our ages, we felt more comfortable at home.

I am glad now that it all happened as it did. We learned to be humble and not on top or in front of anyone. It is always better to stay back and let someone else take the lead. If I had to choose from all the people in the world, I would take my own father and mother. I was taught to live as if we had a depression every year. Should we have another one, what would today's young people do, living on a small lot with a large family and quite a few of them not even having a garden?

## A Good Memory Lesson

FORGET each kindness that you do
As soon as you have done it;
Forget the praise that falls to you
The moment you have won it;
Forget the slander that you hear
Before you can repeat it;
Forget each slight, each spite, each sneer
Whenever you may meet it.

REMEMBER kindness that is done
To you whate'er its measure;
Remember praise by others won
And pass it on with pleasure.
Remember every promise made
And keep it to the letter;
Remember those who lend you aid
And be a grateful debtor.

REMEMBER all the happiness
That comes your way in living
Forget each worry and distress
Be hopeful and forgiving;
Remember good, remember truth,
Remember heaven's above you;
And you will find, through age and youth
That many hearts will love you.

*H. Skinner*

# PART 2 -

# LIVING COMFORTABLY ON NEXT TO NOTHING

*I know that birds have little birds*
*And frogs have little frogs*
*That pussy cats have little cats*
*And dogs have little dogs.*

*That proper minks have little minks*
*And fish have little fishes*
*Then why don't sinks have little sinks*
*Instead of dirty dishes?*

*Author Unknown*

# CHAPTER 2 -

# RUNNING A HOUSEHOLD ON NEXT TO NOTHING

*Crumbs from the Rich Man's Table*

During the Depression, the men got laid off, the factories shut down, and people had to make do the best they could. Today, there is unemployment money, as long as it lasts, but that isn't forever. It is important to know how to get along when there isn't any money.

We hear many people complain about the cost of food these days, but they keep right on buying and of the best too. For myself, I can say the prices don't bother me so very much. If it's too high for my pocket book, I don't buy it.

I can truly say I live from the crumbs of the rich man's table and have almost all my life. Bones others would throw away can be cooked and the bits of meat taken off. The gristle, fat, and skin can be fed to the cats or dogs. The broth makes a wonderful stock for soup. Add onion, carrot, dry beans, or whatever one has available. Celery and parsley give it extra zest and nutrition.

There is so much wasted food it makes one shudder. Some of us older folks who went through the Depression must bite our tongues and not mention the waste, or we will be laughed at. It used to be when butchering a hog very little was wasted. The small intestine was cleaned to put sausage in. Now people pay $12 a container to buy sausage casings at the store and throw the intestine away rather than clean it. The head was worked up and put in scrabble. Today, I've seen more than one head buried so the dog wouldn't drag it onto the front lawn and chew on it. The fat taken from intestines was rendered and made into soap for washing clothes.

Some say they can't cook without meat, but we were poor when I was growing up and also when I had my own children. We had many days without meat. Doing without it is not harmful, but I am not saying it's poor food either. Too much fat is not good for people, be it from any kind of animal, but some older folks are too thrifty to throw it way. So they save it and make homemade soap.

The following recipes and tips are included here for the purpose of informing the reader how things were done in years past, when many household cleaners and needs, such as window cleaners, paste, soap, furniture polish and the like could not be bought at the store. These are the recipes we made up in the home and used.

## WINDOW CLEANERS

Our good friend, vinegar, was our number one staple for windows. We mixed 1/3 cup cider vinegar with 2 pints of water. An old worn diaper was used to wash and crumpled newspaper was used to dry and polish the window. We had no paper towels at that time.

The window cleaner I use today is also very easy to make and works very well. It is made of 1/3 cup rubbing alcohol mixed with 2 pints of rain water. I mix the concoction and put it into a spray bottle to use.

## HOME-MADE SOAP

Collect all your grease from whatever source, including home-canned meats, to use for soap making.

If your grease comes from pan frying and contains salt (bacon grease, ham grease, etc.), cook the grease in double the amount of water. Remove from the burner, let it cool overnight, and then skim off the fat. Use this grease in any of the recipes below.

A small amount of commercial laundry detergent is added as a water softener. Orris root or sassafras may be added to give the soap a nice smell.

Some people believe soap turns out better if it is made during the waning cycle of the moon.

Here are two recipes for homemade soap, both of which will do a good job.

### Home-made Lye Soap

1.  Dissolve 1 (6 oz.) can of lye crystals in 4 pints of rain water. This mixture gets very hot while dissolving, so always use stainless steel, glass, or pottery containers and keep your hands away from it.

2.  Melt 7 lbs. of hog lard, cow tallow, or any scrap of unsalted grease.

3.  When lye and grease are at the same temperature, slowly add the lye to the grease at the rate of about a cup at a time (don't measure, just guess) and stir with a wooden spoon or

paddle. Pour and stir, pour and stir until all is mixed.

4.  When the lye and grease are completely mixed, add 1/2 cup kerosene, 1 cup commercial powdered laundry detergent, 1 cup chlorine bleach, and 1 cup Borax® (as a softener). Stir slowly with a wooden spoon or paddle until all is mixed and dissolved. This takes about 1/2 hour of stirring at times, but when it starts to thicken, pour into prepared molds, again using only glass, stainless steel, or crockery. I use my 8 x 13 layer cake pans. Keep it at room temperature until the following day, then cut into soap-sized rectangles and stack checkerboard fashion to cure. These should be ready to use in two weeks. Store in a dry attic.

5.  If you want a nice scent, add sassafras or other oils. However, the kerosene gives it a very Naphtha-like odor and nothing else really is needed.

## Cold-stirred Soap

1.  Stir 12 oz. of lye crystals into 2 1/2 pints cold rain water. Stir with a wooden spoon until the lye is completely dissolved. (The dissolving lye crystals will make the water very hot.) Let it cool to luke warm.

2.  Melt 12 lbs. unsalted hog lard or suet to lukewarm.

3.  Stir lye solution slowly into the warm lard.

4.   Then add 1/2 cup kerosene to the lard mixture. Stir until well blended.

5.   After the mixture is well stirred and blended, it will start to thicken. Pour into earthenware, wood, steel, or glass molds. Leave for two days or until set, then cut and remove from container to dry as in the recipe above.

Once we had the soap, we were ready to wash clothes. On wash day, first we would find sticks, old boards, dead limbs, etc. and lay them on a pile by the black iron wash pot. Mom would bring the white clothes out, put them in the pot and fill it with cold rain water, then dump in a cup or two of shaved homemade soap slivers.

The next step was to build a fire under the kettle and bring the clothes to a boil. After the clothes had boiled for a while, we would take the stomping stick, lift the boiled clothes out into a pail, and dump them into the wooden tub of the hand washer. More rainwater was added until there was enough to make the clothes move around nicely. The lid was closed, and we would take hold of the handle and push back and forth until we had counted to 100. Now the clothes were clean, so we would turn them out through the hand-powered wringer into another wooden tub filled with rain water with a little bit of bluing added. This was a hand wringer, and the bluing was hard balls. We would tie one of the bluing balls in a piece of cloth and pound it fine, then just dip cloth and all into the rinse water until it was just blue enough. We used no bleach, no softener, commercial cleaning fluid or flakes, but a whiter, softer wash one never saw, and the smell was out of this world. Of course the drier was our old friend "Sol" (sunshine) and Mother West Wind breezes. When dry, most everything was folded and put away as was. This was truly wash and wear, except for a few Sunday clothes, which, being mostly cotton in those days, had to be ironed. We would set our three sad irons on our kerosene or wood-burning stove and heat them until they sizzled when touched with a wet finger. In no time the clothes were ironed, and the wash all put away.

But wait. We were poor and lucky if we had one sheet to a bed and a pair of pillow cases if we were really lucky. So on wash day, the beds would be stripped and when the sheets were dry, they were put right back on for the night. Needless to say, we only washed on bright days.

To kill soap or detergent scum after washing, we added cider vinegar to the rinse tub.

## Soap for Chapped Hands

Lye soap, when properly made, will not cause your hands to chap. Instead, what does chap hands is going outdoors without wiping your hands dry and then hanging clothes to dry. No matter what kind of soap you use, this will leave your hands rough and chapped. The following recipe can help relieve chapped hands and soothe rough, weathered skin.

1. Melt 2 lbs. mild, unscented hand soap

2. Add 1 lb. honey and yolks of 2 eggs beaten together

3. Stir in 1/4 cup Borax®

4. When thoroughly melted and stirred, remove from heat. Pour soap mixture into pan or mold. Add fragrance - oil of lavender, oil of geranium, etc. just before it sets, while it still pours. Let set twenty-four hours, then cut, stack, and age as described for home-made soap.

Here is a good **HOMEMADE WHITENER FOR COTTONS:**

1. Pour one gallon hot soft water in plastic bucket.

2. Add 1 cup of powdered automatic dishwasher detergent, and 1/4 cup of liquid chlorine bleach. Stir well.

3. Add garments to be whitened and soak 1/4 to 1/2 hour. Then wash as usual.

4. Rinse in water to which 1 cup of vinegar has been added.

For nylon or man-made fabric, water must not be so hot. I keep a close watch and as soon as clothes or curtains are white, I take them out of the solution and immediately put them in the washer with hot water and wash them. Rinse in vinegar water.

* * * * *

Many of the household cleaning products available in the store at high prices are made out of simple, inexpensive ingredients which we can make just as easily at home. Here are recipes for some.

## HOMEMADE GLUES

### General Purpose Paste

This is the paste we used to make:

2 tbsp. flour
1 tbsp. sugar
1 tbsp. powdered alum
1 cup water
a few drops oil of cloves or other clean-smelling spice oil

Mix flour, sugar, and alum in a small portion of the water. Heat the remaining water to boiling in a one-quart pan. Add flour mixture at just before the boiling point. Stir with spatula until clear and thickened. Add oil and pour into a quart-size bowl to completely cool. Cover with cloth while cooling to prevent skin from forming on top. Store in covered sterilized jar.

### Quick n' Easy Paste

Today, we go to the wallpaper department of the store and buy a small 2 to 3 ounce box of powdered paste (not wheat paste). It will make an entire dish pan full of nice clear paste at a cost of less than $3. Leftovers keep indefinitely if stored in a glass jar. This paste is nice for school use.

### Cherry Gum Glue

Another good glue can be made from the gum that exudes from cherry trees. Boil this gum in a little soft water. This makes very good glue.

## FURNITURE POLISH

Here are two recipes:

### Recipe 1

> 1 qt. warm water (rain water preferably)
> 2 tbsp. vinegar
> 2 tbsp. good cooking oil or cedar oil

Put in jar and shake well. Soak soft rag with polish and wipe furniture well. Then polish with dry cloth.

*Recipe 2* is good for keeping old furniture from drying out.

> 1 cup linseed oil
> 5 cups turpentine
> 1 cup vinegar

Mix and shake well. Bottle. First wipe furniture with warm water and then with a tablespoon or two of polish. When dry, polish with soft cloth.

## HOMEMADE VARNISH REMOVER

Dissolve two tablespoons of dry lye crystals in 1/2 cup of water. When dissolved, add to 1 qt. of thin starch. Paint on old varnish. This will soften the old finish so it can be scraped and wiped off.

Another recipe for varnish remover uses 1 cup turpentine and 2 cups ammonia. Mix. Then brush on the old finish. When all old finish is removed wipe with a vinegar solution.

## HOUSEHOLD CLEANSER

1 cup ammonia
1/2 cup vinegar
1/4 cup baking soda

Mix and dissolve in pail of warm soft water. Wash walls, varnished woodwork, and furniture.

## MILDEW REMOVER

1/2 cup vinegar
1/2 cup liquid bleach
2 qts. water

Soak cloth. Rinse well in clear water with 1/2 cup vinegar added.

## FERTILIZER FOR HOUSE PLANTS

My mother made her own fertilizer for her house plants as follows:

1 tsp. salt peter
1 tsp. Epsom salts

1 tsp. baking powder
1 tsp. ammonia

Mix thoroughly in 1 gallon warm water. Give plants a good watering once a month. Never water plants with cold water. Between times water with chlorine-free, room temperature water.

And finally, a "REMEDY" FOR COCKROACH-ES: Elderberry leaves strewn on the floor or in cupboards where there are cockroaches will cause them to leave.

* * * * *

There are many more recipes, but these are enough to give you an idea of what a housewife had to do before things were made and sold in stores, and before we had power washers and pumps. So be thankful for the things we have to work with in this day of plenty!

If you are interested in doing more with homemade soap, you might want to look for Ann Branson's book, *Soap-Making and Enjoying It*, which was published in 1975 by Workman Publishing Co.

*My wish is that I could smell the sweet aroma of my grandmother's pantry just once more. She has long gone to her reward, but childhood memories linger still. What are the smells of long ago? Well, there were spices and pickles, the acrid smell of cheese and freshly churned butter, of molasses and possibly something freshly baked like rhubarb pie or a pan of gingerbread.*

*Her jellies were jewels of different colors, not in regular jelly glasses but in long stemmed goblets topped with paraffin and set among her good dishes in the dish cupboard.*

*Dried herb teas and dill hung in bunches from the highest shelves among other seasonings like possibly garlic and onions and dried red peppers.*

*Sassafras roots were chipped or crushed and then dried and kept in a big glass jar on the top shelf along with glass jars of maple sugar cakes.*

*No tin cans of food were bought in grandmother's day. Salt and white sugar were store-bought commodities. Also coffee at times, but it came in whole beans that were ground at home in the coffee grinder, and was only ground as used so it would not lose its pungent flavor. The grinder then would give off another delicious aroma to mingle with the rest.*

*And here in another tin we find a plug of Grandpa's tobacco, used only when he needed something to quiet his nerves. At times of stress, he would cut off a piece the size of a hickory nut and pop it into his mouth and that seemed to clear the air.*

*But now the aromas of old have gone the way of all things along with the pantry itself, and in their stead we have the aroma of foods never heard of in Grandmother's day. The smell of exhaust fumes, smog and etc. But let's not ruin the memories of old with mistakes of the present!*

Written by a farm girl then and a farm girl still. Emma Byler, September 18, 1986.

# CHAPTER 3 -

# MEMORIES OF GRAND-MOTHER'S PANTRY

Some fine foods come out of our kitchens, such as jams, jellies, pies, and breads. But we also, especially in the early days, had to make from scratch many of the basic kitchen essentials, such as yeast, poultry seasonings, and baking powder which we can buy easily now and take for granted. Here are some of the recipes.

### HOME-MADE YEAST
(And Sourdough Bread Starter)

1 pint hops
2 gals. water
2 tsp. salt
1 cup nice light brown sugar
3 lbs. potatoes
1 cup flour

Start in on a Monday morning by boiling the hops in the water for 1/2 hour. Strain off the water into a crock or stainless steel canner and let this tea become lukewarm on the stove (not hot). Add the salt and sugar.

Mix the flour with some of this warm liquid until smooth, then stir it into the rest of the liquid and let it stand. On Wednesday, add the boiled and mashed potatoes. Stir well and let stand until Thursday, then strain and put the liquid in stone jugs (glass jugs will do) with cloth covering. Leave the corks or caps quite loose. Stir the yeast occasionally and keep at room temperature.

This should be made two weeks before using and will keep any length of time, improving with age. Keep in a cool place when storing. Shake jug before pouring out what you want to use. Remove cap and place palm of hand over jug mouth and shake well. One-half cup liquid equals one yeast cake. When you remove this liquid yeast, replace with an equal mixture of flour and water. Today we use granulated yeast from the store, but this works just as well.

## HOME-MADE BAKING POWDER

8 oz. tartaric acid
8 oz. bicarbonate soda
1 lb. rice flour

Sift 6 times and keep in an airtight container.

## POULTRY SEASONING

1 cup dried crumbled sage leaves
2 cups crumbled dry parsley leaves
1 tsp. onion powder
2 tbsp. salt
1 tsp. black pepper
1/2 cup ground rosemary
1/4 cup ground marjoram
1/2 tsp. ground ginger

Combine all ingredients and place in small jars. Label with directions to add 1 tbsp. of herb to 1/4 lb. of butter as a rubbing over fowl, hen, turkey, or goose when roasting. The same portion may be added to bread stuffing.

Little bags of this seasoning make nice gifts for friends during the holidays.

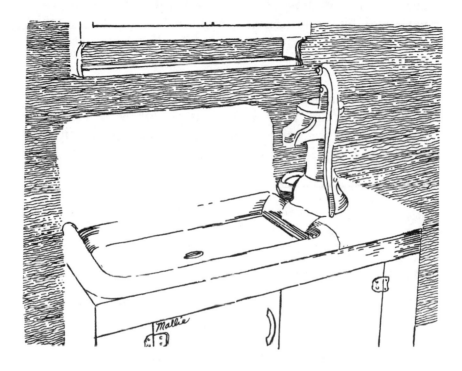

When the children were growing up, we had many meatless meals, but later, as they grew to teenagers and were able to help with finances, we had canned meat and hamburger. So, I would make spaghetti sauce and stews with meat rather than without.

One day one of my sons asked, "Why don't you make 'good' spaghetti anymore?" (He meant without meat!) Well, of course I told him that was the way I made it then because we were poor and couldn't afford to buy meat. So he said, "Well, let's make it the 'poor' way again!" Also, in those later years when we could afford to have real butter instead of margarine on the table, the children wanted to know where the 'real' butter (meaning the oleo!) was.

When money is tight, it is sometimes hard to keep meals interesting. Here is the recipe for **MEATLESS SPAGHETTI** and several other low-cost, nutritious recipes my children enjoyed so much during the years when we had very little money.

1.  Cook pasta in salt water as usual. Add 1 tbsp. vegetable oil to cooking water to keep the spaghetti from sticking together and also to keep the pot from boiling over.

2.  In a heavy sauce pan, sauté 1 whole onion and 1/2 cup finely chopped celery tops. When clear, but not brown, add 1 quart tomato juice[1] or whole canned tomatoes. Cook until thick, and

---

[1]   The tomato juice I can contains garlic, onions, celery, and parsley, in addition to the tomatoes. I cook the ingredients until everything is very soft, then put it all through a Victorio® juicer before I can it. I process ten minutes at 10 lbs. pressure, or twenty minutes in a water bath canner. You could substitute an equal amount of canned tomato/vegetable juice cocktail or add garlic to canned tomato juice.

then pour over or mix in with the pasta. Serves four.

## POOR MAN'S RIVVEL SOUP

1 qt. milk
2 tbsp. butter
pinch of black pepper
1 cup flour
1/2 tsp. salt
1 egg, well beaten

Add butter and pepper to the milk and bring to a boil in a two-quart saucepan. Combine flour, salt and egg. Rub flour, salt, and egg together with the hands until it forms small lumps. Sprinkle these lumps into the boiling milk. Simmer on low heat for 5 minutes, season with salt and pepper to taste, and serve. Serves four.

## RICH MAN'S RIVVEL SOUP

4 cups chicken broth
2 cups corn (canned or fresh)
1 cup flour
1/2 tsp. salt
1 egg, well beaten

Bring broth to a boil. Make rivvels the same way as in the recipe above, and sprinkle the lumps into the boiling broth. Add corn. Simmer for 15 minutes. Serves six.

## SIMPLE EGG NOODLES

2 whole eggs
1 tbsp. cold water
flour

Beat eggs well and add water. Knead in flour by hand until no more will be taken up by the egg mixture and you have a very stiff dough. Put through a noodle cutter if available. If not, roll out on a floured board as thin as possible. Put one piece of rolled dough on top of another and roll up in jelly roll fashion. Cut across roll at the desired width. Use immediately, or unroll and spread on cookie sheets to dry. Do not salt until cooking, as this will draw moisture and cause noodles to mold.

## SHEPHERD'S PIE

This is another poor man's recipe. Mother made her own "biscuit mix" for  this vegetable pie.

1.  Line a 10-inch pie pan with pastry made from the homemade biscuit mix or store-bought, powdered buttermilk baking mix, prepared as for biscuits, but rolled as thin as pie dough.

2.  Cook a cup or two of canned, fresh, or left-over meat of any kind and season to taste. Save broth, if any.

3.  Cook and season to taste 1 potato (diced), 1 cup peas, 1/2 cup carrots (diced), 1/2 cup celery (sliced fine). Save broth of potatoes and carrots, add to meat broth, and thicken slightly.

4.  Finely dice 1 small onion.

5. Put the meat, diced onion, and vegetable mix into the pie shell in alternating layers until all is in the pie shell.

6. Pour at least 1 cup of the meat and vegetable gravy over the meat and vegetables. Cover the pie with slit pastry, and bake until pastry is nice and brown in a medium (350° oven) about 30 minutes.

## HOME-MADE BISCUIT MIX

9 cups all purpose flour
1/3 cup baking powder
2 tsp. salt
2 tbsp. sugar
2 cups shortening

Mix like pie dough. Store in refrigerator. Keeps six weeks.

For biscuits, use 3 cups mix with 2/3 cup milk. Mix and knead 15 strokes. Roll 1/2" thick, then cut and bake for 15 minutes at 450° - 475° for regular biscuits.

## THREE GALLON COOKIE MIX

1. Mix together, one ingredient at a time:

   5 eggs
   5 cups brown sugar
   3 cups margarine
   3 cups milk

2. Mix together:

   6 tsp. baking powder
   4 cups all purpose flour

3.  Add 3 tsp. baking soda dissolved in 1/2 cup hot water and 2 tsp. vanilla to the dry mix and blend.

4.  Combine the dry and wet mixtures and blend. Add more flour as needed (it takes approximately 8 cups) until dough is right for cookies.

5.  Drop dough on greased cookie sheet, or roll out, using enough flour on the board so it rolls nicely.

6.  Bake at 400° for 12 minutes, or until brown.

\* \* \* \* \*

Even though ready-made cereals are easy enough to get, I still like this home-made breakfast cereal better than anything we can get at the store.

### HOME-MADE BREAKFAST FOOD

2 qt. buttermilk
1 qt. molasses (cane)
1 tbsp. soda to 1/2 cup very hot tap water
1 tsp. salt
2 tbsp. vanilla
1 tbsp. maple flavoring
12 cups graham flour

Mix in the order given. Pour about 1 inch thick into lightly greased loaf pans. Bake for 40 minutes in a 400° oven. Do not let it get too brown. Watch closely. When just done and while still a little warm, rub through a piece of 1/2" hardware cloth. Then put on cookie sheets in a 200° oven until well dried. Store in airtight containers until used. This is a large batch (1 gallon or more).

One of the most common cookies we make now, but couldn't afford to make during the Depression are **BUSHEL COOKIES:**

    5 lbs. sugar (brown preferred)
    2 1/2 lbs. lard
    2 lbs. seeded raisins
    12 eggs
    2 lbs. chunky peanut butter

Mix well and add:

    1 qt. milk
    2 lbs. rolled oats
    5 tbsp. baking powder
    5 tbsp. baking soda
    1 cup baking molasses
    6 cups flour

Mix well and drop by the spoonful on greased cookie sheets. Bake in a 400° oven for 12 minutes.

When we were living on the farm with a lot of chores, I didn't always have time to bake a cake for school lunches or snacks. So one or the other of the younger children would say, "I'll bake one. Just tell me how." So a new cake was born. We called it **OUT OF MY HEAD CAKE** because I would just tell them what to put in without looking at a recipe. Here it is:

1. Put 2 eggs in a bowl. Add 1 1/2 cups white sugar and 3/4 cup lard. Beat these three items real good.

2. Then add 1 1/2 cup milk and 1/2 tsp. salt. Do not stir.

3. Put on top of this, 3 cups flour and 3 tsp. baking powder.

4. Now, "beat like billy!" Add 1 tsp. vanilla and beat again.

5. Grease a 9" x 13" pan and dust with flour. Bake at 375° until a toothpick inserted in the center comes out clean.

As I remember, this cake was rather solid, and it was served with pudding if we had it for supper. When used for school lunches, we put powdered sugar icing on it. Son Allen was the one who usually baked this cake. One time the teacher discovered that he had made it, so he had to share with her! This was rather embarrassing for a boy.

There was nothing fancy in cooking when we lived on the farm. We made plain white cookies we called **AUNT FANNY COOKIES:**

1. Begin with:

   5 cups sugar (1/2 of which may be brown sugar)
   4 eggs and 2 1/2 cup soft lard

2. Mix these ingredients well and set aside.

3. In a separate container, add 2 tbsp. cider vinegar to 3 cups of rich milk and let stand 5 minutes. Then dissolve 3 tsp. soda into this milk mixture.

4. Add the soured milk to the creamed sugar and egg mixture, alternating with 6 cups flour. Stir well, adding 2 tsp. vanilla.

5. Dough may be dropped on a baking sheet, or chilled and then rolled out. If you roll the cookies, you may need to add more flour.

6. Bake until nicely brown in a 400° oven.

This makes a big pailful of cookies.

Salads were also important in our family, and this dressing was used when we worried about calories:

## NO CALORIE SALAD DRESSING

1/2 cup wine vinegar
1 clove garlic, crushed
1 tbsp. fresh parsley, finely snipped
1/4 tsp. oregano or tarragon
1/2 tsp. salt or substitute

Shake well and pour over salad. Keep refrigerated.

This **CUCUMBER SALAD** is a nice, easy summer salad.

2 cucumbers, sliced thin
1 onion, sliced paper thin
1 green sweet pepper, sliced thin.

Sprinkle 1 tsp. salt over the vegetables and refrigerate 2 or 3 hours. Rinse off the salt with cold water. You may need to rinse twice to get rid of most of the salt.

Dressing:  3/4 cup cream or creamy style salad dressing
1 tbsp. sugar
1 tbsp. vinegar
pinch of pepper (optional)

Pour over the vegetables and serve cold.

## SPLIT PEA SOUP WITH HAM

2 ham hocks or large ham bone
2 large onions (minced)
1 lb. dry split peas
1 tsp. salt
1/8 tsp. pepper

Simmer meat in 2 quarts water for 30 minutes. Add split peas and cook slowly an additional 1 1/2 hours. Cut meat into small pieces, discard bone and gristle, and return meat to soup. Add salt and pepper. Add more water if necessary. Makes 10 cups.

This recipe comes straight from the farm using our own home-cured ham. Sometimes if we had an unexpected guest or two, Mother would add 1 or 2 cups of milk, which did not spoil the soup in the least.

## REAL OLD-FASHIONED MINCEMEAT

3 quarts chopped apples (cored but not peeled)
4 quarts cooked meat, boned and ground with a coarse chopper blade
1 lbs. raisins
1 1/2 cup cider or 1/2 cup vinegar and 1/2 cup water
2 1/2 tsp. cinnamon
2 1/2 tsp. allspice
3-4 cups light molasses or the same amount of brown sugar.

Mix all together and cook until hot. Put the hot mixture in pint jars and cold pack for 20 minutes. It keeps for years. Makes 8 quarts. One quart makes two pies.

## POOR MAN'S MINCEMEAT

Mincemeat can be made with no meat also, using green tomatoes:

1.  Pour boiling water over 4 quarts of sliced green tomatoes and let stand until cold. Drain. Repeat three times.

2.  Mix together:

    4 quarts sour cooking apples, cored but not peeled. Grind with medium blade
    2 lbs. raisins
    1 cup vinegar
    6 tsp. cinnamon
    3 tsp. cloves
    5 lbs. brown sugar
    2 tsp. salt (or more to taste)

3.  Drain tomatoes and add to the rest of the ingredients. Cook until tender. Pack hot into pint jars. If it seals on its own, no processing is needed. If the jars don't seal, process in water bath for 10 minutes. Makes 8 quarts.

An excellent **BASIC HERB SEASONING MIX** (which can be used as a salt substitute) is made as follows:

    1/2 tsp. cayenne powder
    1 tbsp. garlic powder
    1 tsp. dried leaf basil
    1 tsp. dried leaf marjoram
    1 tsp. dried leaf thyme
    1 tsp. dried leaf parsley
    1 tsp. dried savory
    1 tsp. onion powder

1 tsp. finely ground black pepper
1 tsp. rubbed sage

Grind the basil, marjoram, thyme, parsley, and savory to powder in blender or by rubbing through a screen by hand. Blend all ingredients in a bowl, then fill salt shaker as needed. Excess may be stored in glass jar with tight lid. Use this instead of salt.

## SAUSAGE SEASONING FOR 50 LBS. OF GROUND MEAT

1. Combine 1 1/2 cup salt, 1 1/2 cup brown sugar, 2 tbsp. black pepper, 1 1/2 tbsp. ginger, 1 tsp. sage, and 1 tsp. red pepper.

2. Mix with 50 lbs. of ground meat. Test by frying up a patty, then adjust seasonings to your taste.

3. Stuff mixture into sausage casings or bags made of muslin.

4. Hang and smoke 3 hours, 1 hour at a time. I do this by making a fire in the morning in the smokehouse and letting it go out. I repeat this on the second and third mornings.

5. After smoking, remove muslin and slice. Sausage can be canned in a pressure canner at 10 lbs. pressure for 60 minutes.

For those planning on having a crowd over, you might like to know how we go about it. Here is my shopping list for my sixth daughter's wedding dinner (noon meal). This is enough to feed about 300 guests, which was considered a large Amish wedding from the 1940's to the 1970's:

35 white leghorn hens
9 gallons peeled potatoes
3 gallons gravy
15 loaves medium home-made bread for dressing

6 quarts frozen peas or lima beans
3 gallons gelatin (add pineapple, marshmallows, etc.)
small bushel peeled apples for baking
8 medium heads cabbage, 1 bunch celery, 1 onion, a little red pepper or carrot for color
6 lbs. dried prunes
15 layer cakes, besides Eck (bridal) cakes
15-18 pumpkin or custard pies
1 3 lb. and 1 6 oz. can of coffee
20 lbs. Swiss cheese and 30 lbs. ham to pass for both the noon meal and supper

For the wedding supper (evening meal) we needed:

30 lbs. hamburger for meat loaf or 20 quarts home canned meat
2 large dish pans potato salad
2 gallon diced cooked potatoes, 1 large onion, celery, etc.
4-5 lettuce heads
1 large canner noodles (8 lbs.)
3 gallons mixed fruit
3 gallons cooked pudding or 12 batches date pudding
15 berry pies

We sat 160 people at once, 40 each on the porch, in the bedroom, in the living room, and in the kitchen.

Today's weddings (1980's and 1990's) are much larger and costlier too. Anywhere from 400 to 600 guests are invited, and we expect at least two-thirds of them to attend. For the noon meal today, we need:

80 fryers
8 stewing hens to make 2 canners (7 gallons) of chicken gravy
12-14 gallons of peeled potatoes
24-30 loaves of homemade bread for dressing
24 lbs. frozen peas
4 gallons gelatin with fruit and whipped cream topping added
5 gallons cole slaw, with onion, celery, carrot, and red pepper
15 layer cakes (beside the Bridal cake)
25 pumpkin or pudding pies for noon meal
2 three lb. cans of coffee
1 regular sized jar of instant coffee
30 lbs. of cheese and 50 lbs. of cold ham to pass

The modern day wedding supper requires:

65 lbs. of hamburger for meat loaf
4 gallons cooked and diced potatoes for salad
12 lbs. dry noodles to make 2 large canners full
8 batches of date pudding with sauce
12 apple and 12 cherry pies to be served with ice cream

The **WEDDING PUNCH** recipe is made from

1 46 oz. can orange juice
1 46 oz. can pineapple juice
1 46 oz can grapefruit juice
1 12 oz. can frozen lemonade
1 qt. gingerale

Keep all on ice until just before serving and serve over ice cubes.

Some of the fine things which came out of our kitchens in days past include jellies, pies, etc. made from wild plants we collected or from scraps of plants which would normally be thrown away. Here are some of the more interesting recipes.

## QUINCE HONEY

1. Boil 2 lbs. sugar and 1 pint water for 5 minutes without stirring. Leave lid on for the last 3 minutes.

2. Peel, pit, and grind 2 large quinces. Add to syrup and boil 10 minutes more. Put in jelly jars and seal.

## PEACH SKIN JELLY

It is a shame to throw away the peach skins after canning peaches. Here is something you can do with them:

1. Cook 3 quarts of peach skins with 2 quarts of water. Toss in 2 pits and boil until the skins are soft. Pour through cheese cloth and save 3 cups of juice.

2. Add 1/4 cup lemon juice and 1 pkg. of powdered fruit pectin and put in a 6 quart (or larger) kettle. Bring to a boil.

3. Add sugar according to the recipe on the pectin box and bring to a full rolling boil. Boil for 1 full minute.

4. Skim and pour into hot sterilized jars. Yields 4 1/2 cups.

There are many plants that volunteer in the garden which make good food as well as medicine. **DANDELIONS** are a good example. The young dandelion leaves, collected before the flower buds appear, make a delicious salad. Use 1 qt. of washed shredded greens and 4 hard-boiled eggs. Make flour gravy by browning, in a frying pan, 2 tbsp. flour in 1 tbsp. of bacon grease. Add about 1 cup of water or milk to thicken slightly. Add 1 tbsp. vinegar to the cooled gravy, toss into greens, and serve. This can also be served over boiled potatoes. The fresh or dried ground root, collected in early to late fall, can be steeped in boiling water as a tea which is good for kidney and liver problems. Roasted, it makes a very good coffee substitute without caffeine.

Another volunteer found in the garden is the ground cherry. If you plant ground cherries once, they will come up year after year. These make delicious pies if you leave them until the husks are dry and the cherries are golden yellow.

## GROUND CHERRY PIE

Line 9-inch pie tin with unbaked pastry dough. Make the filling with:

2 cups ground cherries
1 cup sugar
2 tablespoons of instant tapioca or 2 scant tbsp. corn starch

Cover with slit pastry top. Bake at 425° for 50 minutes.

Dill is another plant that comes up in the garden every year. Here is a never-fail **DILL PICKLE** recipe:

1.  Make a brine syrup out of

    1 1/4 cups sugar
    4 1/4 cups vinegar
    1/2 cup coarse salt
    4 cups water

2.  Wash and sterilize pint or quart jars. (If I have 6-8" long cucumbers, I leave them whole and use quart jars, but one can also slice them and pack them in pint jars.)

3.  Put two heads of dill in each quart jar or 1 head in each pint jar. Add one small onion, one clove of garlic, and 1/2 tsp. pickling spice to each jar.

4.  Wash and dry cucumbers and pack them whole or sliced in the jars.

5.  Heat brine until boiling. Pour over cucumbers in jar. Put on lid and screw down tight.

6.  Place the filled jars in a water bath and bring the water to a full, rolling boil. Turn off heat and leave jars in hot water 5 minutes before removing.

7.  Jars must be sealed. If syrup is left over, it may be saved in the refrigerator for later use.

In the late summer, when one gets tired of keeping ahead of the weeds, many of those weeds may be turned into good salad items. Tender shoots of dandelions, mustard, and sorrel may be found underneath the bean plants or growing right along with the beets or carrots. Cut them up fine and put in with your other tossed salad greens.

Beet tops also make excellent greens. Wait to thin your beet row until the biggest plants are as big as a radish. Pull these and clean them, and they will give you a nice mess of beet greens and roots. Season with salt and a little vinegar before serving.

# CHAPTER 4 -

# FOOD FOR FREE TO NEXT TO NOTHING

### *Operating an Efficient Garden*

Memories of Grandmother's garden are imprinted deeply in my mind, and now they bring sweet thoughts of the bountiful harvest. First of the harvest was the big stems of rhubarb. It seems to me that rhubarb never gets as big anymore. Grandma's rhubarb was as thick around as a broomstick. Now all we see is the spindly little stems tied together in bunches at the supermarkets. Next was the asparagus. When I was a child, I would shy away from it, but today it is a rare treat indeed. And next the little red jewels from the currant bushes to be made into jelly. My grandmother put the wine-colored jelly into her glass goblets to be covered with paraffin. These were then set in the dish cupboard among the good dishes until they were used on the holiday tables. And does anyone make quince jelly anymore? Or was it quince honey? The aroma of ripe quinces permeating through the house gives it a truly delicious smell.

Then while working in the garden, out of some nook or cranny would come the heady aroma of mint tea from some volunteer plants that seemed to shy away from Grandma's hoe. These herbs were gathered, tied in small bunches, and hung in the attic to dry for winter enjoyment.

Pennyroyal, peppermint, and spearmint were all favorites. Catnip was always saved for colicky babies as was fennel.

Grandmother would do her hoeing early in the morning and do her canning by noon. Afternoons were spent in the front porch rocker, mending or reading or doing handwork that was not too strenuous.

So why do we have to rush, rush, rush until late hours these days and do no more than they did then? They had plenty to eat out of their gardens and didn't have to go to the stores. They raised their own potatoes, onions, beans, and apples and stored them in the cellar bins made for this purpose. Some were wrapped in paper and packed each in its own little spot. Some needed damper places (celery and cabbage), others drier places (onions, pumpkins, and potatoes), each giving off aromas all their own and mingled together to bring to mind holiday dinners to come. These vegetables would keep until eaten, or some until spring when a new crop would be ready. I've tried all my life to follow in the path my grandparents made for us. I failed a good many times but hope my grandchildren will have sweet memories of me and my pantry, cellar, garden, and that the path I leave them will not be too crooked to follow. May the Lord bless and keep us all.

While I was growing up, money was not only scarce; there was just none to be had. But, life didn't stop. We had to live somehow, so we did. A big garden was a necessity, even if the weather was cantankerous and failed to cooperate.

First of all, my father would plant potatoes. Sometimes as early as Good Friday. Some people still do plant on that day, rain or shine or snow, and these same people always plant lettuce on St. Patrick's Day and come up with the first lettuce too. Now for potatoes, we need a loose loamy soil. Ground plowed for the first time in many years should only be planted to corn or beans, any kind of beans. If the ground refuses to raise beans, then it is in bad shape indeed. How about a good coating of animal manure? Cow, sheep, goat, pig or chicken manure? Yes. Horse manure? No! The weed seed the horse eats will pass right through the digestive tract of the horse and come out prime to grow.

We never wasted wood or water, no matter how plentiful. This advice came from our thrifty grandmother, who said, "Whoever is wasteful of wood and water will not be thrifty of anything else." When the weekly washing was done with home-made soap and a hand washer, the children would carry the cooled wash water out to the garden in pails and give each cabbage, tomato, potato, and other plants a dipper of good soapy water. As I remember it the Depression years were also hot, dry years which brought the chinch bugs, army worms, and grasshoppers in swarms, but good old wash water wasn't to their liking (and it was free at that).

The basic thing which gives me with a sense of well-being is a garden to provide me with my year's supply of food and decoration. From there I can have all the produce canned and put away, and a supply of the herbs I need to heal and beautify, dried and stored away in labeled jars.

Although we dress plainly and our homes are not decorated with man-made things, we raise our spirits and put color in our homes with God-given gifts -- plants and flowers, both fresh and dried. Artificial flowers are taboo.

There are lots of little tips which make gardens more successful. Here are some of them.

## Preparing and Planting the Garden

- In late February or early March, start seeds indoors in peat pots. When they have three or four leaves, transplant them. If they get too big, set them where it is cool -- 40-60 degrees. This slows growth down and makes them sturdy. It basically hardens the plants.

- Before using horse manure on your garden, make sure it has gone through a heat. We leave it set in a very compact pile for a year before spreading. Adding a pan of wood ashes now and then is good for the soil. Also add weeds, clippings, garbage (but not too much). Sawdust should only be added to a compost pile if it has cured by sitting at least a year. Anything that rots is good on the compost pile.

- Plant fine seeds and seeds for root crops such as carrots, parsley, and beets in the better part of the garden. Beans, corn, squash, and cucumbers can be planted in the hard, lumpy part. Tomato and cabbage plants can use rich humus also.

- Be sure to add a handful of wood ash to each hill of the cabbage family (cabbage, broccoli, cauliflower, and brussels sprouts) while planting to get rid of root maggots.

- In a fair year, a bushel of seed potatoes should yield ten bushels or more of potatoes. To make sure they do, dust the seed potatoes with lime and don't spare the soap suds if available. (Soap suds, not detergents!)

- To keep your radishes free of worms, sprinkle enough salt in the row along with the seeds so it looks a little white.

- A shake of salt in each hole with melon and cucumber plants or planting an onion or garlic in each hill will keep the bugs away.

- A mixture of moth flakes (1 tbsp.) to a little lime in each cucumber or melon hill helps also. The mixture should not touch the seeds.

- Everything planted in the garden that bears fruit above ground should be planted as the moon's cycle approaches full moon. Anything bearing fruit below ground such as potatoes and carrots should be planted during the waning cycle of the moon. Winter potatoes should be planted during either the last quarter of the old moon or first quarter of the new June moon.

### Plant Food for Raspberry or Grape Plants

- Mix 1 gallon sifted wood ash, 1 gallon white lime, 1 handful of sulphur powder and 1 handful Epsom salts. Mix well and put one large handful around each plant in February, March, April, and also in the fall.

### Companion Planting

- Plant onion and garlic plants among the melons and cucumber vines and squeeze them to release their odor when hoeing in the garden.

- Plant sage and rue together.

- Planting dill near tomatoes deters tomato worms.

- Plant summer savory with beans.

## Protecting the Garden from Predators and Parasites

- Tobacco makes an excellent insect repellent. Soak cigarette and cigar butts into a brown tea. Soak ground around plants to get rid of lice, bugs, and cutworms. Tobacco juice may be sprayed on plants for aphids and other bugs.

- To keep raccoons out of gardens, lay loosely-crumpled newspaper throughout the patch. Anchor with rock or dirt clod on one corner. The "news" scares them and they will not walk on the paper. You can also spread worn, dirty socks or other old, dirty clothes throughout the garden patch. Coons do not like the human smell. Burning oil lanterns in a corn patch will also do the job.

- Strewing pennyroyal plants around where ants prevail will get rid of them.

- To destroy bugs on squash or cucumber vines, dissolve a tablespoonful of salt peter in a pail of water. Add 1 pint of this at the roots when planting.

- For grubs around peach trees, water roots with the above salt peter solution. One tablespoon to 6 quarts of water.

- Herbs such as catnip, thyme, sage, feverfew, and hyssop repel various insects. Make into a strong tea and spray plants.

## *Maintaining the Garden*

- Keep the soil loose by cultivation. Pull and hoe weeds after each cultivation (weekly).

- Mulch tomatoes and large plants when they get too big and wide to allow the cultivator to pass between the rows.

- Rabbit, sheep, and goat manure are very good for making manure tea to water house and garden plants. This also makes a very good dry fertilizer, as the whole pellets will be a "time released" fertilizer when watering the plants.

- To keep cabbage from bursting when it grows too fast, cut off some side roots with a spade or butcher knife thrust into the ground.

- Lime, ground cayenne pepper, black pepper, and fine wood ash mixed together will make a very good dust for any worms or insects.

- We discovered that sprinkling salt on snails will kill them.

## *Troubleshooting*

- If melons and pumpkins rot, they need lime.

## Harvesting and Storing

- To keep root vegetables in the basement over winter, take five-gallon plastic buckets, one each for red beets, carrots and turnips. Fill buckets with roots and then top them off with sand loosely placed over the top. Set in cool place in basement and vegetables will stay nice and crisp. Cover may be set loosely on top.

## Folk Wisdom about Gardens

- Never cut thistles before St. John's Day (Mid-August).

- A warm June brings an early harvest.

- Eat sage in May if you would live long.

- Creeping under a thorn tree when a lightning storm is in progress is the safest.

- If the oak trees leaf out before the ash, it will be a wet summer.

- Onion skins very thin;
  Mild the winter coming in.
  Onion skins thick and tuff;
  Coming winter cold and ruff.

- Cumin seed makes good bait for traps and tames horses.

# CHAPTER 5 -

# THE LITTLE NICETIES

Herbs can be used to refresh and beautify the home. Here are some of the items I make.

## A NICE SACHET FOR DRAWERS OR CLOTHES CLOSET

Take:

1 thin-skinned orange
2 oz. more or less whole cloves
1 tsp. ground cinnamon
1 tsp. ground orris root
A dab of ground allspice

Prick the orange with an ice pick. Stick in cloves as close together as you can without splitting the orange skin between holes. When the orange has been completely covered, roll in ground cinnamon, orris root, and allspice. Take a square of nylon net big enough to draw around orange. Tie with bright ribbon. Hang in closet for nice clean, spicy smell. Make a few for gifts too.

## FRIENDSHIP POTPOURRI

2 cups peony petals
1 cup rosebuds
1 cup chamomile flowers
1 cup linden flowers

1 tbsp. allspice
4-5 drops patchouli oil

Dry all petals, buds, flowers, etc. Use a screen propped on brick to give circulation all around. Drying takes from 2-10 days. When dry, blend petals and oil in a ceramic bowl. When well blended, store in an airtight container.

## SACHET BAGS

Combine 1 oz. each of powdered cloves, caraway seed, nutmeg, mace, and cinnamon with 6 oz. powdered orris root. Put up in fancy lace and calico bags and sew shut. These make nice gifts. Hang in closet or lay in drawers. These fragrant sachets also repel moths.

## MAKE A ROSE JAR

When your roses are blooming, gather petals before the sun is high. Spread them in 1/2 inch layers on paper, sprinkle with salt, and let stand in shade. Ten days after the last petals are added to the others, add 1/4 oz. ground cloves and 1/4 oz. ground mace. You may also add one drop of rose geranium or 1 oz. of cologne over the mixture. Put in a jar and you will have a delightful rose fragrance all winter.

## EASTER EGG DYES FROM PLANT MATERIALS

Choose farm-fresh eggs and hard boil as many as you will need.

### Table of Dyestuff

**Orange**    yellow onion skins, dried sassafras root, bedstraw roots and oats.

**Red**    crab apple flowers, cranberry fruit, red peony petals, red tulip flowers, beet roots.

**Yellow**    ground apple tree bark, buttercup weed flower, forsythia flower, whiteskin onion, yellow tulip flowers, yellow pansy flowers, ground tumeric with vinegar.

**Green**    flowering crab apple (leaves and bark), iris flower, blue and yellow pansy flowers mixed, black oak bark shredded. Using alum as mordant makes a beautiful green.

**Blue**    red cabbage head (shredded), blueberry fruit (pale grey blue), red onion skin, iris, (blue flower parts only), pansy flowers, violet flowers.

| Tan | coffee (stewed as a strong drink), tea leaves (stewed strong) red maple bark (rosy tan). |
| Brown | flowering quince bark, walnut hulls, ground paprika, bark of the scarlet maple. |

Coarsely chop or shred one or more cups of fresh material or two or more cups dried material such as bark, roots, and spices. Put dyestuff in muslin bag tied at top.

Use glass, enamel, or stainless steel dye pots. Never use aluminum or copper.

Add 4 cups of tap water if it is not too hard (rain water is better). Simmer dye stuff for 30-90 minutes. Use 1 tsp. alum per cup of dye or 1 tbsp. white vinegar to set the dye.

Raw eggs may be put into the dye bath and simmered for 20 minutes for deeper colors. Precook the eggs for lighter colors. Turn eggs frequently. Dry on paper towel. Try your supermarket for onion skins.

Cloth may be dyed the same way.

## DOUGH CHRISTMAS ORNAMENTS

For those who like to make their own Christmas ornaments or table decorations, here is a recipe for dough which can be formed into permanent ornaments.

1. Mix together 2 cups all purpose flour and 1 cup salt.

2.  Start adding 1 cup water. (It will take more or less, depending on the humidity.)

3.  Stir into ball and knead 7-10 minutes. Work in as much flour as possible, as one needs a firm dough. Food coloring may be added with the water.

4.  Cut out or form into desired shapes. Bake on cookie sheets preheated to 325°. Bake until rock hard. A piece 1/2" thick will take 1 1/4 to 1 1/2 hours to bake.

Pricking with needle will help so it does not bubble. Cover with at least three coats of paint or varnish to keep moisture out.

# PART 3 -

# AUNT JEMIMA'S PLASTER
# AND
# OTHER HOME REMEDIES

*When a teacher asked the class to write down what they had learned about the human body, this is what one boy wrote:*

*"Our body is divided into three parts, the branium, the borax, and the abominable cavity. The branium contains the brain, if any. The borax contains the lungs, the lights and the heart. The abominable cavity contains the five bowels -- A, E, I, O and U."*

# CHAPTER 6 -

# THE HEALING POWER
# OF SIMPLE THINGS

When I was young, we had no money for medicine or doctors, so we had to use what was available. Most home remedies use plants, because we believe God puts healing and everything man needs into plants.

It is important to remember, however, before using any home remedy, to consult with your physician when you are sick and discuss these home remedies with him, or at least get an accurate diagnosis of your ills from him. His diagnosis is essential. Money spent for diagnosis is never misspent. It is very important to be treating the proper disease.

It is amazing how common, old-fashioned household things can be useful in improving health. One wonders how people came up with such things. What instincts or knowledge of the workings of common household chemicals did they have that prompted combining the various herbs, waxes, rosins, soaps, and salts in the ways that they did to effect cures?

Sometimes, the cure is as simple as just going for a walk! Those suffering from headaches and other stressful conditions, such as muscle spasms, leg cramps, etc., try walking briskly one-half hour each morning and again in the evening.

When we were all sick at once, Mother would clean the house in the morning until everything was fresh and aired, then she would sprinkle sulphur powder on the hot stove for a good fumigation.

Some remedies sound really strange, but they seem to work. Why, I don't know. At least they won't hurt anyone, so you might as well try them and see if they help. These include such things as:

- For a sore throat, taking off your dirty socks at bedtime and tying or pinning them around your throat.

- Making a poultice of bread and milk to draw out soreness and poison in wounds. *(See page 99)*

- For removing ticks from the skin, placing a piece of tape over the insect. *(See page 127)*

and one I read in an old newspaper, in which a woman wrote:

*"My husband had rheumatism in his knee. The doctors said there was nothing to be done but to stay off of it. One evening, our phone rang and it was the granddaughter of an old friend. After chatting a few minutes, she said Grandma would have used green cabbage leaves. Put them on the knee, tie them up and leave them on all night.*

*We put them on at 10 p.m., and at 2 a.m. my husband woke me and said he could not stand the drawing anymore. He would put some on the next morning. The leaves were dried like old newspaper and by morning, his knee was back to normal. All this 16 years ago and never any pain since. This doesn't work for all types, but it did miracles for him. "*

The remedies in the following chapters make use mostly of foods and plants that are readily available to those who want to try them.

Naturally, the remedies included here are not all that exist. There are many more, but these are the ones, mostly, that I have learned and that my family has used over the years, which I pass on to you for whatever good they might be. I leave it to others much wiser than I to write about all of them. In the Appendix are references to more wide-ranging herbal books which I have found useful.

# CHAPTER 7 -

# THE HERBAL MEDICINE CHEST

Home remedies only work if the ingredients for them are in the home when you need them.

Most of the plants I use for home remedies I either grow or collect in and around my back yard. Most are brought in, tied in bunches, hung from the rafters until dry, and then crumbled and stored in bottles or paper bags.

The plants I grow for my herbal medicine chest include:

*sage, feverfew (leaves and flowers), lovage, catnip, pennyroyal, peppermint, orange mint, dill, green and blue cabbages (for leaves), celery, snap beans (leaves and shells), rosemary, marjoram, thyme, pumpkins and watermelons (for seeds), onions, and garlic.*

The rest of what I need for remedies, I either collect from the wild or buy from such places as Chupp's Herbs and Fabrics or Indiana Botanic Garden (see Resources in the Appendix).

In summer, I collect:

**For their dried leaves:** *boneset; orange, spear and apple mint; catnip; shepherd's*

*purse; dandelion; horsetail grass; blue ver-
vain; and the wide and narrow-leaved plan-
tains.*

I usually collect these plants just before they flower
for the greatest strength.

**For their roots:** *comfrey, blackberry, dandelion, ginger, bloodroot, calamus (sweet
flag), and golden seal.*

These are usually dug in late summer and sometimes
into early fall.

**For their flowers:** *elderberry, feverfew, corn silk,
and tansy.*

The flowers are dried by hanging them from rafters
in paper bags. They are then stripped from the stalks and
put in jars.

In fall I collect:

**For their leaves:** *wintergreen, raspberry,
strawberry, blueberry, pennyroyal, chick-
weed, ground ivy, live-forever, peach, and
snap bean. Lobelia is collected for the
whole plant.*

**For their roots:** *calamus, sassafras, and
sometimes dandelion.*

**For their flowers:** *chamomile and yarrow.*

**For their fruits, berries, and seeds:** *flax,
pumpkin, watermelon, fennel, cranberries,
blackberries, sumac berries and snap beans.*

The fruits and berries are collected when they are ripe.

I also can a good supply of *blackberry-cranberry, blueberry, elderberry, and grape juice.*

Whatever herbs I can't find, I can mail order from Chupp's Herbs and Fabric or Indiana Botanic Gardens listed in the Appendix at the end of this book. I also buy the following from the store: **pulverized charcoal, lemon juice, honey, vinegar, beeswax, rosin, camphor, and alum.**

With these plants and other aids in my cupboard, I am ready for practically any ailment my family may develop.

# CHAPTER 8 -

# THE CURATIVE POWERS
# OF ORDINARY FOODS

Ordinary foodstuffs can help prevent sickness and also often double as medicines.

Thinking back over the years about our eating habits, I'd like to write a few words. Probably not all that I write will be scientific, but it won't be harmful either.

Scientists are now discovering that eating vegetables may help avoid cancer. Even smokers have less chance of contracting dreaded lung cancer if they eat vegetables and get good, nutritious meals. A very important subject to teach in all schools, be they Amish or Yankee, would be meal planning and teaching the children (not just the girls) why they should eat good, balanced meals.

It is important to eat the right foods, including lots of vegetables, both steamed and raw. Lots of the problems we have today with poor health and overweight come from eating the wrong things, especially fats. Lots of calories are added to food through the butter and gravies prepared with them as a sauce or dressing.

When my children were growing up, the first time we had cauliflower on the table fixed with plain milk, cheese, salt, and pepper, my grown son said, "What's that? I don't want any. It don't smell good." But I persuaded him to try just three bites and if he didn't like the vegetable,

I'd never ask him to eat it again. He tried it and later asked for seconds and ate that before anybody else had a chance to get their seconds!  Since then, he really likes it.

Mothers, encourage your children to eat just one spoonful of peas, beans, broccoli, or whatever vegetable you may be trying. I've heard mothers say to their children at the table, "No, you don't like it, I'm sure you don't," which only shows she didn't like it herself and wasn't going to teach her children to eat it either. And probably the mother didn't get good, nutritious food at home. Some mothers think that if they keep baked goods and pudding on the table, they are being good cooks!  And some complain about the price of groceries, but if you notice, they have two or three bags of candy and gum with their groceries. And two or three times a day they give candy or gum to keep the children quiet. It is also given as a reward for doing minor jobs. These children are forever having toothaches and being taken to the dentist.

The importance of having plenty of greens in the diet can't be stressed too much. Green vegetables, collected and eaten fresh while all the vitamins are still in them, are one of the best cures for even some very serious ills. Some time ago, a newspaper reported about a lady who came from Russia with legs so black with gangrene that the doctors threatened to remove them if they didn't improve. Each day, as she sat in her wheelchair in her brother's garden, she would lean over and pick anything green she could get hold of. One day, the story said, she even ate a bouquet someone brought!  Within a short time, the gangrene was healed. I don't know for a fact that this is true, but greens, eaten in large quantity, have always been the folk remedy for poor circulation and some cases of gangrene.

Eat milk, butter, or cheese at least once a day. A green vegetable should also be eaten at least once a day —

the greener, the better. Some young people are very wasteful in this area. Not that they realize it, but at weddings,
some of us older and wiser ones cringe at all the things
being thrown away by the cooks. Celery leaves with hearts,
outer leaves of lettuce and cabbage, fruit juice. Unless they
are dried and wilted or badly bruised, these are usable.
Drying celery tops and crushing them for later use to
crumble into soups or gravy is very good food, and all these
scraps have lots of food value and very few calories.

Onions have medicinal values in addition to being
a good food. When we were growing up, we were always
afraid when children had the croup, because there weren't
the antibiotics which we have now. Mom would put onion
plaster on them. Mom made the plaster by placing goose
grease or olive oil in a pan on the stove, slicing an onion
into the pan and sautéing it enough to wilt the onion and
bring out the juices. She then put all this in a muslin bag
on the person's chest. This would cause a sweat and pull
out the croup. It smelled awful, but it did the trick.

To stop a hacking cough, you sliced an onion,
sprinkled a little sugar over it, put it where it was warm,
and let the juices ooze out. Then you would put one or two
drops of ooze on some sugar and place it in the mouth. It
stopped the cough but wasn't too popular with the children!

What the children did like for a cough, however,
was the juice of half a lemon, a tablespoon full of honey,
and 1/2 tsp. of butter stirred in to make it kind of greasy,
and then put in the back of the throat. This tastes much
better than onion ooze on sugar!

Eat lots of onions and garlic, raw or cooked. This
kills germs.

Honey is another item we used as medical help in our home. Dad would spot a tree with bees in it in the late summer and when zero weather came, he would cut the tree and take out the honey, keeping the dark and light combs separate. Dark honey is much stronger. When using dark honey, mix it with white corn syrup to give it a milder flavor. Do **not** give either raw honey or products containing honey to babies less than one year old.

For bedwetting, 1 tsp. of raw honey taken before retiring cured members of my own family.

I had a very good friend who, when she was not feeling well, would make a drink of 1 tbsp. of vinegar and 1 cup of cool water and it would ease her stomach.

Every so often, I'll take a tablespoon of cider vinegar in one-half glass of water and drink it as a general tonic. Sometimes I'll put a spoon of honey in it. It deters the appetite and helps if one has kidney trouble, hay fever, or a variety of other ills. I also seem to lose weight if I do it every day for two weeks or so.

The value of cranberries in the diet cannot be stressed enough. Not only are they very good food, but the crushed berries make a very good poultice for wounds, such as dog or cat bites. Animal bites should have first aid first, by a doctor if severe. But the soreness and swelling can be reduced by a poultice of the berries. The poultice will also draw out poisons.

Cranberries will also help cleanse the system when eaten and helps indigestion conditions. Some feel you will not be infected by prevailing illnesses such as flu and the grippe if you use them during the winter. And it is well known by most people today that urinary and bladder infections may be relieved by drinking cranberry juice.

Beans are also good for treating kidney troubles and dropsy. Boil navy or pea beans until partly soft. Drain off the cooking liquid and have the patient drink 1/2 cup several times a day. Also pods of kidney or green beans are said to help in these cases. Boil pods of green beans until partly tender, drain off water and drink 1/2 cup of the liquid at a time. This is also recommended for gout.

Sorghum syrup in your diet is said to help dry scalp and dandruff, and molasses and butter are helpful for dry coughs.

Vitamins, minerals, and other dietary supplements, in my estimation, are used and pushed too much today. If one eats a well-balanced diet, these supplements are rarely necessary. The only reason I use vitamins is because I live alone, do not cook for myself and, so, need supplements to make up for this loss. There are several vitamins that our family has used with very good results, however.

- *Vitamin C* (500 mg.) and zinc (50 mg.) is a very healing combination for general use that now even some doctors recommend after an operation.

- *Rutin* has been very useful in helping those suffering from hemorrhoids. Men and boys who work in the woods, and others who do hard labor, are prone to getting hemorrhoids. I knew one who the doctor said had to have an operation who bought a bottle of rutin tablets at the drugstore. Before he had finished half the bottle, his hemorrhoids were cured. It can't hurt to try. If a full bottle doesn't cure them, then it's time to go for other help.

- *L-lysine* works for shingles, cold sores, and any herpes-type sore. One time my mother had a cold sore inside her nose for over a year and nothing would cure it. Before she had used one bottle of L-lysine pills, the sore was gone.

- *Zinc*. A 30 mg. pill can be taken internally each day. Zinc mixed with sheep lard and used as a lotion, rubbed well into the hands and feet, has cured very dry and cracked hands and feet. Be sure to wear gloves and/or socks to bed when you are using this. Use zinc until you can taste "tin" on your tongue, then stop a while.

If your legs ache and you have cramps in the muscles, you may need more calcium, lecithin, Vitamin C and a whole list of B vitamins, beginning with B-1. If you drink a quart of milk each day and eat a wide variety of green and yellow vegetables laced with lots of onion and garlic, you will probably not need any of the above vitamins.

The very best way to stay healthy, I think, is to eat the plant foods that the Lord has given us at the time they are in their prime. For example, in spring we eat dandelions to clean the poisons out of our system which have built up over the winter. Rhubarb, which cleans mucus and acid out of the liver, comes into season next. We make it into a sauce and eat it every day. This is followed by strawberries, and then all the fresh green vegetables which come from our garden as they become ready, eaten at their greenest. If you eat all these things in season as they come along, you will go into the winter healthy.

# CHAPTER 9 -

# GENERAL TONICS

The herbs we most commonly used, which can be broadly classed as general tonics, include:

- *Boneset* - 1 tsp. of crumpled boneset leaves to 1 pint of boiling water was our favorite for many ailments. I have never had it fail for me for flu or colds. It is very important to use it as hot as one can stand to drink it as soon as the first symptoms are felt. A cup a day for a week does no harm. It can be sweetened with a little honey or lemon, but the bitter taste does no harm and soon one does not mind it.

- *Golden Seal* - Put 1/2 teaspoon powdered golden seal root in 1 pint of boiling water and stew it a bit. I buy powder from Katie P. Hershberger, who advertises in the *Budget* (See Appendix). This is one of the most valuable home remedies. We use it as a hot tea when the first sign of sore mouth and throat appears. Dad would also chew the root as a remedy for his peptic stomach.

- *Calamus (Sweet Flag) Root* - is a remedy for upset stomach, gall stones, gall bladder attacks, stomach pain, or bilious feelings. Chew a piece the size of a pea and swallow the juice. This is good for acid indigestion and especially gas, as it sweetens the stomach.

- *Chamomile Tea* - Steep 1 or 2 teaspoons of dried blossoms in a pint of boiling water. This is another favorite which we use for upset stomach and diarrhea and is also good to relax a person. I drink it warm before going to bed and find it helps me to unwind and brings on a refreshing rest. It is also wonderful for colicky or fussy babies. For them, sweeten 1 cup with 1/2 or less tsp. of honey, and put it in their bottle at the same temperature as milk.

- *Dandelion leaves, flowers and roots* - A good mess of dandelion greens made into a warm salad is a wonderful spring tonic and is good for kidney problems, because dandelion greens and dried, powdered dandelion root are one of the best diuretics known. Dandelion is also good for diabetics.

Each spring, Dad would make up a batch of dandelion wine. This wine was only used for medicinal purposes, such as for hot toddies and so on. It was also one of Dad's bases for his bitters. He would fill a bottle or jar with his own blend of roots, berries, some dandelion wine, and the tea mentioned below. Dad would drink a few small sips of this brew to perk up his heart when it was beating too slowly.

Other herbal teas important to me as general tonics include: *red clover blossom tea, corn silk tea, sassafras tea, and ground ivy tea.* These also are very good for detoxifying the blood, especially for painters exposed to lead.

Dad had a long spouted coffee pot which held about a quart. This was his brew pot. Sometimes just plain bone-set tea was brewed in it. But often times, blue vervain was added for nerves, and/or chamomile blossoms for the same reason. Wild cherry bark was added for a tonic. This was known as the "bitters," and Dad never had to tell us twice to leave it alone!

## AUNT JEMIMA'S PLASTER

I had a maiden auntie,
Jemima was her name.
She used to make a plaster
That brought her lotsa fame.
She made it out of everything
and other things too;
The principal ingredients were
mucilage and glue.

### Chorus

Mutton, tallow, beeswax,
Aunt Jemima's plaster.
When you tried to pull it off,
It just stuck faster.
Hard times, good times,
Triumphs or disaster,
A friend would never stick as fast
As Aunt Jemima's plaster.

\* \* \* \*

When Mother had the rheumatiz
And Father had the gout,
Aunt Jemima's plaster would
pull the trouble out.
We used it for the measles,
For croup and chicken pox,
And Brother used to use a piece
For holding up his socks.

Us children wore a plaster
To keep away the cough;
They put it on in winter time,
In spring they took it off.
When it came to peelin' time
We hollered and we cried;
When they jerked the plaster off
It took away the hide.

\* \* \* \*

Now my Aunt Jemima
She has passed away and gone,
But the memory of her plaster
Still will linger on.
She used to stick it on us
Every place that she could find;
Now recollections of it
Are sticking in my mind.

\* \* \* \*

Aunt Jemima's dead and gone
And when she went to rest,
She wore her finest plaster
upon her gentle breast.
Now if Aunt Jemima has a mortal
soul to save,
The plaster's gonna pucker up
and jerk it from the grave.

# CHAPTER 10 -

# POULTICES, PLASTERS, and SALVES

Page 98 gives the words of a song, "Aunt Jemima's Plaster," which has been handed down through several generations. It was taught to me and I have since passed it along to others. It shows in one way how important plasters were in helping to cure ailments and how we felt about them!

Poultices, plasters, and salves were used primarily for drawing out pain, curing sores, healing wounds of all types, lessening the itch of poison ivy, and curing chest colds, the croup, and pneumonia.

A home remedy we used as I was growing up and also while raising my own children was a poultice of *hot milk and home-made bread*, which, on occasion, was sprinkled with black pepper. This was such a common, everyday cure, yet it never failed to bring things to a head or clean out a deep puncture wound if put on when going to bed. Usually by midnight it had to come off as it was drawing so painfully. I once stepped on a nail that went through my shoe sole into my foot, pushing dirt and bits of stocking in with it. I applied the poultice when I went to bed, and woke up about midnight with a throbbing foot. I took the poultice off and pulled the wound apart and a squirt of pus and bits of dirt came out. So I put it back on for the rest of the night, and by morning it was hardly sore anymore.

Another staple poultice in our family was *"Lily Drum"*. Now, I don't know why the "drum", or maybe my spelling is not the right one. Maybe it was "dram" or some other word for Schnapps, which is what it was made of — the petals of the Easter Lily flower and whiskey. Stuff the petals in a wide mouth bottle, such as a salad dressing bottle, and pour enough whiskey in the bottle to fill it. Then cork it and leave it for several weeks. When it is ready, if someone has a shallow sore, a felon (a painful, pus-producing infection at the end of a finger or toe, near the nail), or other similar infection, lay a lily petal on it and tie it up. Within a short time it will be white and all soreness will be drawn out. I do not remember putting it on a swelling or abscess, however.

A poultice we use for pneumonia is made from:

1 pt. vinegar
5 tbsp. lard
3 tbsp. hard soap (homemade lye soap, cut up fine)

This is put in a tin can and boiled until it gets a little clear. Then we add 2 tbsp. salt, boil some more, add 5 tbsp. spirits of turpentine, and boil a little longer. Soak flannel cloths in this hot solution (as hot as the patient can stand it), and lay them over the chest. Repeat this every 15 minutes for 2 or 3 hours.

The following tobacco salve was also commonly used for pneumonia:

1 pack cheap pipe tobacco
1/2 to 1 lb. raisins
2 lbs. lard

Cook and simmer all together slowly for 3 to 3 1/2 hours. Cool and strain. Put in jar and use as a chest rub or poultice for pneumonia and tightness of a chest cold.

Goose grease and camphorated oil were warmed and used as a plaster on a flannel cloth for our chests. If goose fat was not available, chicken grease or even skunk grease was used instead. Dad would hunt skunks, sell the fur, and we would use the grease to make soap. For plasters, we would rub it on and it would really open stuffy heads. Skunk grease smells awfully strong! It has a milder skunk smell, but it is still there.

With the money he earned from selling skunk hides, Dad bought an oak roll-top desk from Sears. I believe he paid $35 for it. It is still in good repair and is probably worth $1,000 today, which is not a bad return from hunting skunks!

My mother would also use any of these oils for making soap as nothing was wasted at our house.

Other poultices and their uses:

- For blood poisoning, we make a poultice of warm cranberry slush.

- Warm grated raw beets are also a good poultice.

- For corns, soak bread in vinegar and put it over the corn. Keep this on day and night until the corns drop off.

- Slightly cooked onions mixed with camphorated oil or lard, put in a muslin bag and laid on the chest, would break a cold. *(See page 91)*

- Crushed cranberries make a good poultice for wounds, such as dog or cat bites. *(See page 92)*

## HEALING SALVES

Salves are used for cuts, bruises, puncture wounds, and healing generally. If you want to heal a surface wound, put the salve on thinly. If you are trying to draw poisons or inflammation out of deeper wounds, put the salve or poultice on thick.

*Lung Fever (Pneumonia) Salve* has been a staple in Amish medicine chests for years. Our local doctor would often be unable to cure those with pneumonia and would give up. After the doctor said, "I've done everything I can; it's now up to the Lord," we'd put on the lung fever salve and usually within two to three hours the patient would start sweating and the fever broke. The doctor was so amazed that he went to the druggist and told the druggist to keep in stock whatever the Amish used to make the salve. This was fifty years ago, and pneumonia isn't as serious a disease anymore, but the salve still works.

Here is how to make it.

1. Send for a kit of the dry ingredients and camphor from Roose Drug Store, P.O. Box 96, Middlefield, OH 44062 ((216) 632-5201). The price as this is written is $9.25 plus UPS shipping for a 3 lb. package.

2. Heat 12 oz. unsalted lard with the kit's dry ingredients, stirring until completely dissolved and smooth.

3. Remove from heat, add the camphor and the kit's liquids. Stir and cool.

*Aunt Jane's Salve for Healing and Drawing* was in my grandmother's home remedy book from the early 1900's.

4 lumps mutton tallow, size of egg
2 lumps beef tallow, size of egg
2 lumps lard tallow, size of egg
4 lumps rosin, size of egg
2 lumps beeswax (get at drug store), size of egg
3 tbsp. British oil
2 tbsp. fish oil (cod liver)
good sized handful Alder bark (collect or get at herb store)

Another good healing and drawing salve can be made with:

1/4 lb. rosin
2 oz. gum camphor
1/4 lb. beeswax
1/4 lb. sheep tallow
3 oz. homemade soft soap

Melt the first four ingredients together in an old pan. When hot and melted, stir in the soap a little at a time and boil slowly until it is well mixed. Pour into small jars (baby food jars) while still warm. For healing, put a thin layer on a bandage. For drawing out pain, slivers, and blood poison, make a 1/8" thick plaster and apply. Bandage well and leave on all night.

For poison ivy, one remedy was to rub the inside of a ripe banana peel on the itchy area and, of course, eat the banana if you like. In cases where the poison ivy is severe enough to cause an upset stomach, the banana helps to settle the stomach. The other quick cure is jewelweed, which is discussed on page 122.

My grandmother also recorded an *Old Indian Salve* which was made from:

> 1 1/2 lb. bittersweet root
> 1 1/2 lb. black Alder
> 1/2 lb. hops
> 1/2 lb. plantain leaves
> 1 tobacco plug cut in bits

Everything is placed in a pot with enough water to cover. Simmer 1/2 to 3/4 hour or longer. Strain and squeeze out juice. Boil juice down to 1/2 the amount. Add 1 lb. unsalted butter, 1 oz. beeswax, 1 oz. rosin, and simmer over a slow fire until the water is all gone. Use on swellings and sores.

I don't remember ever using it, but it looks interesting!

### Treatment for a Boil

Peel off inside lining of a fresh egg shell, and cover the boil with the lining while it is moist and fresh.

### Good Samaritan Liniment

Mix:
> 1/4 oz. oil of wintergreen (get from drugstore)
> 1/4 oz. oil of cinnamon (get from drugstore)
> 1/4 oz. sassafras
> 1 oz. camphor gum
> 1 quart raw linseed oil (get from hardware store)

This is a very good oil to put on burns. For a bad cough, take 10-20 drops on a little sugar. This may be put up in 4 oz. bottles to share with friends and family.

For minor burns - cover immediately with *aloe vera* ooze. If no plant is available, use lard and flour to make a soft paste. Keep covered so as to shut out the air.

# CHAPTER 11 -

# REMEDIES FOR SPECIFIC ILLS

The following remedies have been used in our family since I was young. Some of the plants used in them have since been banned by the Food and Drug Administration, including comfrey, sassafras, and tansy, as well as pennyroyal for women in childbearing years because it supposedly causes miscarriage. These home remedies are given for information only so that the reader will know what we used (and still use) to help heal our own ills. **They are not given as prescriptions in any way. If you are ill, see your physician. If you use any of these remedies, you do so at your own risk.**

## *Appendicitis*

- Drink a strong tea of untreated alfalfa seed tea: 1 tbsp. seed to a cup of boiling water. Crushing the seed will make it brew quicker. This might help when someone is prone to appendicitis attacks, but do not wait too long before seeing your doctor.

- If we complained of symptoms of appendicitis, Dad would first try the very simplest remedies, like having us go to the top of the stairway and crawl down head first. This was to empty our appendix and it must have worked, as none of us twelve children ever had to go to the hospital for any reason at all!

### Arsenic Poisoning

See Lead Poisoning

### Asthma

- Asthma and aspirin don't mix.

- Cough syrup for asthma: Add 1 oz. wild cherry bark (inner bark) to 1 qt. water. Boil this down to 1 pt. Add 1 cup honey and 1/3 cup horehound candy drops (melted). Mix well and take 1 tbsp. as needed.

- Simmer (covered) 1 cup fresh lard, 1/2 cup sheep tallow and 6 cloves garlic (peeled and cut fine) for 20 minutes. Strain. Cool and put in a jar. Before going to bed, grease the sole of each foot generously. This helps with any bronchial problem. Wear woolen socks to bed.

With any case of asthma, whether home remedies are used or not, you need doctor's care.

### Bedwetting

Remedies we use to stop bedwetting include:

- Drinking a cup of parsley tea three times a day. Use 1 rounded tsp. per two cups of water. If this is too strong, add water.

- Letting the child eat lots of raisins.

- Giving 1 tsp. of honey before going to bed.

- To 1 qt. boiling water, add 1 oz. St. John's wort and 4 tbsp. plantain. Boil down to 1 pint, cool and strain. Add honey to sweeten. Give 1 tsp. morning and night. More would do no harm. This tea is also good for the urinary tract, gravel, and gall stones.

## Bladder Infections

See Kidney Problems below.

## Blood Purifiers and Cleansers

- Drink one cup of warm tea made from any of the following herbs per day for three weeks. Brew 1 tsp. of herb per cup of water.

    ◆ **red clover blossom** ◆ **strawberry leaf** ◆ **elderberry flower** ◆ **dandelion root or leaf (may use more than 1 cup)** ◆ **blackberry leaf** ◆ **blueberry leaf**

My experience is that anything you use as a blood cleaner will thin your blood. If high blood pressure is a problem, it may decrease after using these teas over several weeks.

- Cranberries will help cleanse the system when eaten.

## Blood Poisoning

- This is the salve we call *"Zuppa Shmear"* and use on any wound which could lead to blood poisoning:

    1 oz. white rosin

1 oz. beeswax
1 oz. Venice oil

Melt and mix well into a three-inch bar. When ready to use, melt the end of the bar over the flame of a lamp or candle, and smear onto soft cloth. Put it on the sore as a poultice and cover. Body heat will keep the salve soft. This is used to draw out the poison. Grandmother took a little piece of oil cloth, warmed the stick of salve over a candle or light until it was soft, smeared some on the oil cloth, and put this on an old sore which refused to heal. This would draw out the poisons and let it heal.

### Broken Bones

- Drink boneset leaf tea or comfrey tea made with dried root of the plant. Roots of herbs should be stewed a minute or two to get all the strength. Leaves should be brewed as with any tea. For boneset tea, mix 4 tsp. leaves and flower heads (crumbled) in one quart of boiling water. Add honey to sweeten. This will keep in ice box for several days and can be drunk hot or cold.

The Food and Drug Administration has banned comfrey leaves for human use because it affects the liver, but root tea, taken sparingly for specific ills like broken bones, has cured lots of folks. You have to use your own judgment.

### Bronchitis

- Ground ivy tea (1 tsp. per cup) is good for bronchitis.

## *Bruises*

See Sprains.

## *Burns*

- Put 1/2 tsp. of powdered alum in a 2 oz. bottle of water. Wet the bandage with this and keep it wet.

- Powdered charcoal and cornmeal, made into a poultice, is also good. Cover wound completely and keep bandage wet.

- Apply a coat of honey to cover the wound. The idea is to seal off the air.

- Grated raw potato will draw out heat.

- Cover thickly with *aloe vera* gel or the ooze from a crushed *aloe vera* leaf.

## *Cancer*

- A standard folk remedy for cancer is two cups red clover blossoms, 1 tbsp. ginger root (cut fine) to one quart water, boiled down to one pint. Drain and let liquid cool. Add 1 tsp. extract of bloodroot[1] from drugstore. Add one pint of good whiskey. Mix, put in a bottle, and keep in a cool place. Take one tsp. three times a day until it is all used up. This is also a good tonic to take once a year or when you are run down,

---

[1] Extract of bloodroot comes in a very concentrated form, and it takes 1 teaspoonful of it in this recipe.

because it cleans the blood and keeps the body healthy. It won't necessarily cure cancer, but will improve the bodily condition so that it can more easily cure itself.

### Chapped Hands

- For a soap that helps cure chapped hands, see page 37.

### Colicky Babies

- Two tsps. of crumbled catnip herb to a cup of boiling water, sweetened with honey, makes a soothing tea for colicky babies, and is also soothing for the mother of a nursing baby. Give baby 1/2 cup of this tea in a bottle, as warm as milk.

- Catnip tea can also be made with 1 tsp. to 1 1/2 cups water. At this strength, give babies an 8 oz. bottle between feedings. This makes a happy and contented baby.

- Fennel tea made the same way is also good for a fussy babies. Catnip and fennel may be mixed together in the same bottle.

### Constipation

- Dandelion leaf or root tea and dandelion greens cooked or served as salad are very effective against constipation.

## Coughs, Colds and Flu

- Anything that will make you sweat is good for colds and flu. Boneset tea is one of these. Crumble the dry herb fine and keep in a tightly closed jar out of direct light. This will keep several years and stay nice and green. Brew 2 tsp. of herb in 3 cups boiling hot water and drink boneset tea as hot as you can stand it at the first sign of illness.

Other remedies include:

- Brew boneset, sage, and catnip into a tea. Sweeten with honey. This causes a sweat to break up a feverish cold.

- Combine 1 tbsp. honey, 1 tbsp. whiskey and a little melted butter. Add 3 whole lemons, skin and all, sliced thin, 1 cup sugar, 2 cups hot water, and 2 cups of flax seed. Cook all together in double boiler for 2 1/2 to 3 hours. Strain and cool. Add 1/2 cup brandy. Bottle and use 1 tsp. every hour until relief is found.

- Mix well the juice of 3 lemons, 1 pt. honey, 3 tbsp. maple syrup, and a pea-sized chunk of baking soda. Take as needed.

- Teas made with ground ivy or feverfew, sweetened with honey, are very effective.

- Garlic is very good for respiratory infections. Make a strong tea by steeping 1/2 to 1 teaspoonful of ground and/or dried garlic in one cup of boiling water and drink the mixture while it is still warm.

- For a dry cough - heat molasses and butter and give as needed.

## Depression

- Tea made from blue vervain, valerian root, scullcap, chamomile, or catnip are very good for lifting depression. Use 1 tsp. of herb in 1 cup water, and drink one cup per day.

## Diabetes

- Drink dandelion root and/or leaf tea, and/or eat dandelion greens. Three cups or more a day won't hurt.

## Diarrhea

- Drink one cup of canned blueberry or blackberry juice at least twice a day. Three cups will do no harm. Mother would half fill large jars with blackberries, add water to the rim of the jar, and can them for winter use. We always had lots of blackberry juice. If this did not stop diarrhea, then cooking a handful of blackberry root and drinking the tea from it would surely do it. Roots must be gathered in the fall, washed thoroughly, and dried. This is a favorite remedy for treating cattle with diarrhea as well. *(See page 131)*

- Blueberry leaf, elderberry flower, and raspberry leaf teas (2 tsp. dried leaves to 1 pint water), as well as elderberries, are among the best anti-diarrhetic remedies known for humans. Use 2 tsp. blueberry leaves to a pint of boiling water and drink several cups a day.

- Peach leaf tea is also an excellent cure for diarrhea after everything else has been tried.

- Nowadays people go to the hospital for dehydration brought on by diarrhea or other ills. Back in the Depression, with no money and twelve kids, all we got was large doses of peach leaf, blueberry, blackberry and the other teas and juices listed above. These rough teas cured us. No one ever went to the hospital.

*Dropsy*    (The accumulation of fluid around the heart, in joints and body cavities)

See also Kidney Problems, Blood Purifiers.

- Dropsy can be helped by anything which gets rid of the fluid, including any of the diuretics used as remedies for blood and kidney problems. This includes dandelions in their various forms.

- Make a tea of boiled elderberry flowers and drink a warm cupful several times a day.

- Make a tea of dried cheeseplant (*Malva*), using a cupful of dried herb to 1 quart boiling water. Drink 1 cup three times a day.

- Make tea with 2 tsp. ground ivy to 3 cups boiling water. Strain. Drink daily.

- Licorice root capsules, parsley tea, garlic, and garlic and parsley taken together in capsules are also effective.

### Dry Scalp and Dandruff

- Sorghum syrup added to the diet seems to help.

### Eye Problems

- Blue vervain or eyebright herb teas both make a good wash for sore eyes.

### Flu

See also Coughs and Colds.

- Eating cranberries in the winter will protect you from being infected with illnesses such as flu or cold.

### Gout

- Boil navy or pea beans, or pods of green or kidney beans, until partly soft. Drain off water and drink 1/2 cup several times a day.

- Eat forty cherries of any kind, fresh or canned, each day.

### Headache

See also Stress.

- Sage may be used as a tea, at 1 tsp. per cup, for nervous headaches as well as for flavoring sausages, chicken, and stuffing.

## Head Lice

- There was a time when the druggist didn't have strong enough drugs to kill head lice, so instead of spending $40 for a treatment, we would make a strong concoction of sassafras root tea and wash and rinse our hair repeatedly with it. Now we can buy sassafras oil and this is very good to use the same way. **Warning:** this is to be used on the head only, not to be taken as medicine.

## Heart Problems

- Blue vervain tea is good for the heart, as is rosemary tea brewed 1 tsp. per cup. Blue vervain was one of the plants my father kept in his long spouted coffee pot, but I'm not sure if it was for his bad heart or for nerves!

## High Blood Pressure

- Drink 1 cup of any of the following teas daily. They can be used singly or mixed. Use 1 tsp. per cup boiling water: chamomile, blue vervain, catnip (whole plant), and blueberry leaf.

## Indigestion

- Eating cranberries may help.

- Calamus (sweet flag) root also helps. Cut a chunk of dried root about the size of a pea, chew it, and swallow the juice.

- Dandelion root tea, or roasted dandelion root coffee, will also help against gas and acid pains.

### Itching

- Plain cider vinegar stops itching. Wash the itch with plain water, pat some vinegar on cotton, apply to the itch, and let the air dry it.

- Jewelweed (touch-me-not) is also a very good remedy for itching caused by mosquito bites, bee stings, stinging nettles, or poison ivy and is usually found growing right with or near poison ivy and nettles. Rub the fresh juice of the stem or leaves on the itch.

### Kidney Problems

See also Bladder, Urinary Tract, Dropsy, Blood Purification.

- The tonics mentioned in Chapter 9 were taken in spring to clean the blood and kidneys of poisons after the long winter. Others also were useful in cleaning out the system. These are:

- Teas made from dandelion leaf or root, yarrow, cheeseplant (*Malva*), ground ivy (what the Amish call "Dunkle Rava"), and horsetail grass (*Equisetum*) were used for kidney and bladder problems. Brew 1 tsp. of herb per cup of boiling water. Drink one cup a day, or in the case of dandelions, several.

- Dandelion (greens or the dried, powdered root) is one of the best diuretics known. A good mess of dandelion greens made into a warm salad and dressed with a warm sweet and sour dressing was used as a spring tonic. *(See page 96)*

- Parsley is used for the same purpose. We used it green in salads and soups or dried in many other dishes.

- Dried corn silk is made into a tea for babies if they did not wet for a day or so.

- Dried, ground up watermelon seed was also made into a tea, at 1 tsp. per pint of water, and used for this purpose.

- The cooking water from navy, pea, kidney, or green beans helps with kidney problems and dropsy. *(See page 115)*

- Cranberry juice is also very good for urinary or bladder infections.

### *Lead and other Metal Poisoning (Painter's Disease)*

One can get lead poisoning today not only from paint and paint chips. Lead may also be found in gasoline exhaust fumes, old water pipes, and possibly even cooking utensils.

- Tea made from dandelion, bugleweed, bladder wrack, Irish moss, kelp, red clover, corn silk and/or ground ivy as well as anything else which contains large amounts of Vitamin C (Ascorbic Acid) will help remove lead from the system. These can either be gathered during the summer or bought as capsules through herb stores or herb mail-order catalogs (see Appendix). Make tea of 1 tsp. plant to 1 cup boiling water.

### Leg Sores

- Bathe sore regularly once a day in salt water - 1 tsp. salt to 1 quart water. Today, the doctor says no soaking, but no harm can be done, and it is very healing. Soaking a leg sore in salt water gives much relief.

- One of the best treatments is to sprinkle the sore with golden seal powder and/or use golden seal capsules or tea (1/4 tsp. per cup of water).

- I knew someone once who filled leg sores with canned, mashed pumpkin, and then wrapped bandages around to hold it in place. I don't know if it helped, but it wouldn't hurt to try!

### Liver Problems

See also Kidney Problems.

- Dandelions are one of the best liver treatments known. Use as recommended for tonics (Chapter 9) or as described under Kidney Ailments.

- Rhubarb sauce will rid the liver of mucus and acid.

- Blue vervain, served as a tea (1 tsp. herb per cup of water) is also good for the liver.

### Lungs

- Two tablespoons of cider vinegar added to one quart of boiling water will do wonders for bad lungs. Use this combination in a hot water vaporizer or inhale the vapors from a large bowl or basin.

## Memory

- Rosemary herb was used for many ills, including failing memory and heart tonic. It also is used to flavor beef roast, chicken, and tomato soups.

- Sage, which we use to flavor food, also improves the memory and makes men wise -- hence the name "**sage**" for a wise man.

## Menstruation

See Pregnancy.

- A tea made of 1 tsp. dry crumbled red raspberry leaves to 1 cup boiling water and sweetened with honey, lessens the discomfort of the monthly period. Drink hot, and use no more than 2 cups in twenty-four hours.

## Nursing Mothers

See Colicky Babies.

## Painkillers

- Meadowsweet is aspirin in its natural form. Use 1 tsp. dried leaf to 1 cup of water as tea whenever you would use aspirin.

## Pneumonia

In addition to antibiotics provided by the doctor and the poultices and salves in Chapter 9:

- Drink hot boneset tea twice a day. Drink lots of fluids.

- Make a drink of 3 cups hot water, 1/2 cup lemon juice, and honey to sweeten. Drink this hot, all in one day.

## Poison Ivy

- The juice from the stems or leaves of jewelweed, rubbed on the affected area as soon after contact as possible, will in most cases cure poison ivy, as well as bee stings, mosquito bites, and sting-ing nettle itch.

- A strong wash or tea made from a mixture of lobelia and ground root of golden seal will re-lieve itching. Use 2 tsp. lobelia per cup of boil-ing water, and 1 tsp. of golden seal powder. If you don't have both of these herbs, use either one.

- *Aloe vera* juice, plantain, or dock leaves rubbed on the blisters until green juice appears will stop the itching.

## Poor Circulation

- Eat spinach, cabbage, dandelion (greens and/or powdered dry root), and broccoli -- basically anything that is green and edible. *(See page 90)*

- Take gelatin capsules filled 1/2 full of powdered red pepper with a glass of lukewarm water. This is also good for other ailments. Two or three capsules may be taken at once if you have no ill effects. This is also good for the circulation, if you can stand it. I have also heard that mixing red pepper with lobelia is good.

## Pregnancy

- Strawberry or red raspberry leaf tea may be used until about three weeks before birth only. We always used it up until six weeks before birth then stopped everything except what the doctor advised. The doctor's medicines were always used along with herbal remedies during pregnancy. Black cohosh and blue cohosh teas are also good.

## Puncture Wounds

See Blood Poisoning, Leg Sores.

- Soak puncture wound (such as made by stepping on a nail) in 3 quarts of very warm water in which 1/2 cup Epsom salts has been dissolved. Keep water as hot as can be borne. Then make a poultice of hot milk and bread, and keep it on all night. Next morning, the soreness and poison is usually drawn off. *(See page 99)*

- You can also use golden seal and maybe even mashed pumpkin. *(See page 120)*

## Rheumatism

- Make a tea of elderberry flowers boiled as one would for dropsy and drink a warm cupful several times a day.

- 2 lbs. Epsom salts, 12 lemons sliced, 1 tbsp. cream of tartar. Put in a gallon jug and fill with lukewarm water. Let stand a few days. Shake well. Use 2 oz. a day.

- Cabbage leaves placed on sore joints as a poultice may also help. *(See page 82)*

### Shingles

- Saturate sores with golden seal tea.

- If I had shingles, cold sores, or sores hard to heal such as herpes, I'd use large amounts of L-lysine. Vitamin E oil, dabbed on the sores, is very healing.

### Skin Problems (Rash)

- Make a salve out of pokeberries simmered in lard.

### Sleeplessness

- Elderly people who can't sleep at night or are restless often have a poor diet that lacks protein. Try 1 tsp. of plain gelatin in 1 cup of cold water. Soak 5 minutes. Add 1 cup boiling water. Stir until dissolved. Then put 3 Tbsp. of this in a glass of milk, water, or tea and drink at supper time. A small box of sweetened gelatin dessert, any flavor, made per directions on the box and mixed with the above gelatin is more palatable.

## Sore Throat

- The best thing for sore throat is hot golden seal tea. The sore throat must be caught right when it first starts getting raspy, however, for this to work. Drink it as hot as you can stand it, a cup at night and in the morning.

- A good mouth wash for a sore mouth or gargle for a sore throat is hot salt water.

- Tea made from either blue vervain herb or sage also makes a good gargle.

- There is the old folk remedy for a sore throat that you probably won't believe, but it seems to work. Take off your dirty socks at bedtime and tie or pin them around your throat. Maybe it's the warmth from the sock that causes this to help!

## Sprains, Bad Bruises and Swellings

- For a sprained ankle or arm, make a concoction of chopped plantain and/or comfrey leaves and/or ground comfrey root. Brew in a kettle of hot water to make 1 or 2 gallons. Soak the sore ankle or arm in this as warm as one can tolerate. Keep hot by adding more water.

- A good soak of the feet once a day for about 20 minutes or 1/2 hour in a mash made of plantain (we Amish call this "si ohra blatter" or "pigs ear leaves") and/or comfrey leaves will also help this condition. It can't hurt you to try. One time, when my nephew broke his foot falling off a ladder while siding a house, his foot became so swollen the doctor couldn't put a cast on. Nephew didn't want to stay in the hospital till the swelling went down, so he came home. His mother gathered plantain, cut it up and put it in water as hot as he could stand it. This drew all the soreness and swelling out so that the cast could be put right on.

- Red clover blossom tea is also useful against swelling.

## Stomach Upset

- When we are sick to the stomach, we eat a "milk toast", made by toasting bread, putting butter on it, then crumbling it in hot milk and eating it. Mint, catnip, or chamomile tea, such as is used for stress (see below), also will calm the stomach. Oatmeal is also good. Do not eat rich or spicy foods.

## Stress

- Those suffering from headaches and other stressful conditions, such as muscle spasms, leg cramps, etc., try walking briskly for 1/2 hour each morning and again in the evening.

- Brew 2 tsp. crushed blue vervain leaves and flower heads in 2 cups boiling water. Sweeten with honey. Drink one cup warm before retiring and one cup the next day.

- Mint, catnip, or chamomile tea will serve equally well. Use blossom of chamomile only. Use whole plant for mint and catnip. Crumble 1 tsp.

plant or flowers into 1 cup of boiling water, and drink warm.

### Swelling

See Sprains.

### Ticks

- For removing ticks from the skin, place a piece of tape over the insect. Remove tape and the insect will be pulled out along with the tape. Do not leave the tape on long or infection might result.

### Tumors

See Cancer.

### Ulcers

- To help a peptic ulcer, fill medium-sized capsules with powdered red pepper and take as many as you can stand. Begin with only one or two capsules until your stomach will tolerate more.

### Warts

- Castor oil will make warts disappear if they are kept saturated with it for awhile.

- Vitamin E also seems to work on warts, as well as moles. Rub the oil on them.

- Keep warts covered with clear nail polish. As it wears off, reapply.

## Whooping Cough

I remember well when I had the whooping cough and had it extra hard, so that when I started coughing someone would have to hang on to me so I wouldn't fall on the floor. An extract of chestnut leaves was recommended, but I don't remember the dose.

If infected with this disease, it is well to do some coughing in order to expel the phlegm from the throat and lungs. The medicine we use to help this happen is made as follows:

> 1 lemon thinly sliced
> 1/2 pint ground flax seed from drug store

Simmer slowly in 1 pint water for 4 hours (do not boil). Strain through sieve while still hot. Add enough water to make it back to 1 pint. If necessary, add 2 oz. of honey. Adult dose: 1 tbsp. four times daily, and one additional dose after each fit of coughing. Child's dose: 1 tsp. four times a day and one more teaspoonful after each spasm of coughing.

And then there's one final remedy to finish this chapter that comes under the heading of *Falling Asleep in Church*! I've heard say that taking three ginseng capsules before leaving home will keep you alert until after church. Don't take them at night, however.

# CHAPTER 12 -

# ANIMAL AILMENTS
# AND THEIR CARE

A few thoughts about pets left in the house:

Did you know that people in Bible times considered dogs unclean and to be kept outside. Now don't ask me where one can read all this, but it is my opinion that it is the truth. A dog harbors ten to twenty different kinds of parasites catching to humans. Your doctor or vet can tell you this. A dog's place is outside the house, especially where there are small children in the home. They are not to be cuddled on your lap or on your bed or table.

Pet turtles can also harbor diseases as can pet birds such as parrots or parakeets. This goes for pet cats as well. Rabbits are not usually kept in the house, but one can get a disease known as tularemia from dead rabbits.

The Bible calls only a few animals clean. Yes, I like animals and they are beautiful, but a lot of sickness could be avoided by keeping them outside.

Some of our most unusual pets have been, believe it or not, crows. They came to us during the spring and summer of 1977-78. The first good buddy was Sam. He would drop out of the blue on silent wings, and it seemed everyone was his friend (at least for a while). He would talk, jabber, and make noises until he was sure he had your attention. Then *his* fun began.

While planting the garden, I was harassed until nothing but murder would do, and let me tell you, I'm a mild-mannered person. He would pick out the onion sets, carry away any seed packets not securely anchored under a rock, and spill the fertilizer until gardening was two steps back and one step forward. So I would pretend not to see him until he got close enough to grab. Well, I tried, but ended with a big handful of air at least a dozen times. So I hid a stick along the side of my skirt. Here he comes -- swish, swish, swat, bang -- everywhere but hitting Sam. When it got too hot for him, he'd sit in a high tree with not the usual "caw caw" but the plainest "ha ha ha" one ever heard. His snooping ways finally got him in trouble, however, and he ended up being caught in a trap set for another varmint. So that was the end of Sam.

But wouldn't you know, the very next spring my son came home with a nestling crow -- two beady black eyes, a puff ball of feathers and the biggest black bill one ever saw on such a tiny mite. We named him Jim and spoon fed him bread, milk, and vitamins every two hours until he grew a bit, then twice a day until he was full grown. He would ride to church or town on top of our buggy. A strange noise or sight would send him winging home. His great pleasure was landing on the clothes line full of nice clean wash, picking off the pins and carrying them away and hide them in the eaves. He had a great fascination for fire, heat, or steam. He would get as close to the flames as possible without getting burned and would bask in the heat. He had free sailing to wherever he wanted to go and never paid any attention to his kin flying overhead.

Jim lived in the barn with the animals in winter. By spring he was ill and died soon after. Our lives seemed better and richer, however, for having known both Sam and Jim.

Diarrhea was often a problem with our dairy cows. Just like in people, blackberry root tea also was very effective for dairy cows with severe diarrhea, after the vet had exhausted his medicines for that ailment. Blackberry roots were cooked in large kettles and one gallon was administered to each cow by drenching. Two times in one day should do it. Drenching is done by putting the juice in a long necked bottle and pouring the liquid down the cow's throat. A couple of years ago the farmer two houses down had a cow whose feces were pouring through like water. The vet gave up on it. The farmer went out, dug blackberry roots, boiled them down, and drenched the cow with this blackberry root tea. In three days the cow was cured.

Some other remedies we have found useful for our animals include:

- To repel insects from poultry, dust dried, crumbled pennyroyal leaves into cracks in the roost and elsewhere in the chicken house.

- Tobacco juice made very strong (1 pack chewing tobacco to 5 quarts water) is also a good insect repellent. Pour the juice into the cracks of the roost.

- Washing horses with pennyroyal tea keeps flies and sucking insects from them.

- Washing dogs and cats with pennyroyal tea to rid them of fleas.

- Feeding dogs and cats brewer's yeast and dusting and rubbing it into their fur to rid them of fleas.

A general tonic for horses, which worked well to repel worms was made as follows:

5 lbs. Epsom salts
5 lbs. sulphur
1 lb. salt peter
4 oz. cream of tartar
4 qt. sifted wood ash

Mix well, give 1 tbsp. 2 times a day. Scatter over his grain. To tame and calm horses, try mixing cumin seed in their feed.

To be honest, with some of these remedies, I'd rather have the disease! It seems that the disease bugs would only have to hear what was coming their way to get scared enough to die or run away.

If cows refuse feed and water for days, and the antibiotics vets give them don't work, try feeding them cabbage. One Amishman reported that he started such a cow on cabbage, and right away she'd eat a head at a time, and in two days was back on her appetite for other feed.

Here are three home remedies for calf scours:

• Put 1 tsp. soda, 1 tsp. ginger, 1 tsp. cloves, 1/2 tsp. nutmeg, 1/2 tsp. cinnamon in a bottle and add a cup of warm water. Give to calf. A bit more water wouldn't hurt.

• Add raw eggs to milk for calves at first sign of scours.

• Add 2 tsp. table salt, 1 tsp. baking soda, 8 tbsp. honey or white corn syrup to 1 gallon water, and give to the calf (up to 80 lbs.) all at once each day. Withhold milk or replacer. Several times a day would not be harmful.

For proud flesh (lumps of soft tissue which form over injuries and never quite heal, and so have to be removed for the wound to heal) in humans or animals, bind on a handful (or enough to cover sore well) of brown sugar. Leave until proud flesh is gone. Add fresh sugar if needed.

And finally, if horses chew the top of the manger or other wood in the barn, try the following:

- Sprinkle 1 Tbsp. sifted wood ash on the horse's feed for each meal.

- Sprinkle 1/4 cup vinegar over the horse's feed.

- Finally, and especially for the top part of the manger, put heavy wire along the top. No. 9 will do. Staple it well. Horses don't like the metal grating their teeth.

# PART 4 -

# HAPPY ENDINGS

## Daily Bread

*Though I have always liked to cook*
*And see that folks are fed,*
*The kitchen work I favor most*
*Is making daily bread.*

*I even like the tools I use --*
*The spoon's familiar feel,*
*My own two hands, and mixing bowls*
*Of shiny, stainless steel.*

*I love the smell of kneading bread,*
*The texture of the dough;*
*I love to shape and oil the loaves*
*And place them in a row.*

*How often Jesus spoke of bread.*
*He blessed and multiplied it.*
*He cooked it once by glowing coals*
*With sizzling fish beside it.*

*Scripture after scripture now*
*Is running through my head.*
*I never think of things like these*
*When I am **buying** bread.*

Janice Etter

# CHAPTER 13 -

# AMISH FOLK WISDOM AND HUMOR

You will find that the Amish have a wonderful point of view about life, which they share with lots of humor and sometimes a bit of tongue-in-cheek. Here is a sampling of some I've cut out of Amish magazines and newspapers over the years, which I'd like to share with you. I don't know where most came from, or I'd credit them.

## A BUSINESS DEAL

*My old Aunt Samanthy received $1,000 from Uncle Sam for not raising hogs. I think I'll go into the hog non-raising business myself next year.*

*Now, give me your opinion. What is the best kind of farm on which not to raise hogs? And the best kind of hogs not to raise? I prefer not to raise Razorbacks myself, but if this breed is not good for not raising, I'll be satisfied not to raise Berkshires or Durocs.*

*The hardest part of this business will be keeping inventory on how many hogs I haven't raised. (I had three days of school in my brother's place when he was down with the virus!)*

*Aunt Samanthy is happy about the future of her business. When she raised hogs, her best year was a total of $400. But, think of it, this year she made $1,000 by not raising fifty. On that basis, I would get $2,000 for not raising 100.*

*I plan to operate on a small scale at first, simmering myself down from not raising 100 hogs to not raising 400. Then I will net $8,000. Another thing. These hogs I will not raise will not eat 100,000 bushels of corn and I will also be paid for not raising this corn not to be eaten by the hogs I'm not raising.*

*Naturally, I want to embark on my new venture as soon as possible, so I'm anxious to obtain the necessary forms for keeping my non-hog raising for Uncle Sam. I don't want to be left standing on the outside with a bushel of corn on the shoulder and a hog by the tail because of poor bookkeeping!*

\* \* \* \* \*

Thirty-five years ago when our son, David, was born, our family doctor was engaged to deliver our baby at the home of a midwife. The doctor was overworked and tired as country doctors usually were. When the doctor arrived at 11 p.m., he opened the basement door instead of the brightly lit entrance door, and fell head first down the basement stairs, taking along a jelly cupboard with jelly, pickles, and several cans of molasses.

After the din of breaking glass, scattering tin cans, and splintering wood quieted down, we heard a row of words not meant for publishing. The doctor slowly gathered himself out of the mess and found himself without a scratch.

While the midwife was cleaning the molasses and jelly from the doctor's clothes, I was paralyzed, not daring to have even the slightest pain. But in a surprisingly short time, he was cleaned up and ready for business, with only a little pickly smell about him. Within half an hour, our third son was born. After the doctor left, the midwife went into fits of laughter, but I was too thankful to see the funny side of it.

Giving birth to children is just the beginning, as any mother knows. Here is a little poem I wrote in 1955, after sending five children out the door to school.

## RAISING KIDS

*Off to School*

*From fall till spring vacation*
*We have the awfulest actionation*
*When sending five kids off to school*
*I can stay anything but cool.*

*First in the morning it's peace and quiet;*
*Then they wake up, it sounds like a riot.*
*It's, "Where's my garters, my tablet, my books,*
*My shoestrings, my socks, my dress's not on the hook."*

*They want to know, "Can we have a dime?*
*We haven't had one in such a long time."*
*Now a dime's not much but five times ten*
*Adds up to fifty cents again.*

*When, at last, I shoo them out the door,*
*I feel like falling on the floor.*
*They've borrowed my garters; my stockings are down*
*My shoes are flopping; the strings are gone.*

*My pins they are loaned; my dress it is open.*
*It's really so, I'm not just joking.*
*I turn around to view the mess;*
*It's really no worse than yesterday, I guess.*

*So my kids go to school*
*and get a little brighter,*
*While I stay home*
*And my hair gets a little whiter.*

*Emma Byler (Jonas Em)*

It was while the last five of my ten children were in Mesopotamia Elementary School that I met Marceline and Albert Stevens from Southington, Ohio. Mrs. Stevens had been hired as principal for Mesopotamia Elementary, among the most underprivileged schools in Trumbull County during the 1960's.

Mrs. Stevens was hired right after the race riots in Cleveland, when many black families, mostly from the Hough area, were moving into Mesopotamia. They brought not only their own children, but many foster children as well.

Before Mrs. Stevens took over Mesopotamia Elementary, there had been several male teachers as well as a male principal. All quickly found work elsewhere once they discovered what they were up against, but Mrs. Stevens was not dismayed by the task of having to combine inner-city, Amish, and rural Yankee children in the small school.

There were about 260 pupils in the entire school. About thirty percent were Black, 50% Amish, and 20% local. Many of the Black pupils, aged 15, 16, and 17, were still in the sixth, seventh, and eighth grades. Their knowledge of crime and exposure to violence were far beyond anything the Amish and most local children in their early teens ever dreamt of, yet Mrs. Stevens was determined to see that all the children under her care received an education.

Mrs. Stevens' methods might be judged harshly now, but she needed to let students and their parents know from the start that stern discipline and honest effort was expected of all pupils in Mesopotamia Elementary School. Mrs. Stevens didn't flinch at telling newly-transferred, inner-city students that it was up to them whether they made a success of life or stayed "poor Black," and placed (not passed) all high school age students in the local high school at the end of the year. Her methods worked, as I remember that we had several very honorable black students pass through the school.

Sometimes children were threatened with knives or razor blades that the Black children had brought to school. In Cleveland students had carried these weapons to protect themselves, but Mrs. Stevens would not tolerate such behavior in her school and confiscated the weapons.

When problems arose in the classroom that the teachers were unable to handle, the children were sent to the office to see Mrs. Stevens. Some of them brashly claimed that they would take no punishment from her. This challenge left Mrs. Stevens undaunted. She would offer them a seat and then proceed to read them the rules of "her school." Students were then asked to think over for a few minutes whether they wanted to take punishment from her or be sent home for three days or, in a few cases, possibly forever. Most decided to take their punishment from Mrs. Stevens because the parents or foster parents would do everything possible to keep the children in school.

Some parents resented having their children punished by the principal. On one occasion when Mrs. Stevens came to school in the morning, she was met by a group of irate parents. Mrs. Stevens calmly asked them to be seated while she called the Sheriff, as "I need someone on my side, too." This did the trick! The parents were very willing to settle without calling the Sheriff for help.

So that's the way it was at Mesopotamia Elementary School. At the end of ten years, Mrs. Stevens had truly cleaned up our school in more ways than one and made many lifetime friends among all three cultures.

Albert Stevens was a retired banker when I met him, and a great help in school, running errands whenever needed. Mrs. Stevens brought much money into the school through various government programs. If anyone needed help in applying for these programs, she was the person to see. She unraveled the red tape in no time.

Albert and Marceline Stevens are both gone now, and I miss them. They were very caring people, always sharing what they had before ever thinking of themselves. Mrs. Stevens also helped me out whenever she could. I was hired as cook for several terms, and sometimes I was the substitute janitor at school.

I helped Albert with the house cleaning, the lawn and planting their garden for 18 years. The most beautiful memories I have are of times we'd work hard getting the house sparkling clean, and then he would sit down and play several pieces on the organ. He was a very talented player and played for many a wedding.

Last, but not least, while talking about children:

## A FATHER'S LECTURE TO HIS SON

*Dad had been lecturing his young son on the evils of staying out late at night and getting up late in the morning. "You will never amount to anything unless you turn over a new leaf," he said. "Remember that the early bird gets the worm, my boy."*

*"But how about the worm, Dad?" asked the young man. "Wasn't he rather silly to get up so early?"*

*"My son," replied Dad seriously, "the worm hadn't been to bed. He was on his way home!"*

I could never end this book without telling a story on myself. One time when attending the wedding of a niece in Pennsylvania, we stayed the night, and after eating sweets, sours, and all that goes along with a wedding dinner, sleep would not come, so at a late hour, I went into my mother's room and asked her for a phenobarbital pill so I could relax and go to sleep. She said there was one on the sink in the kitchen where I was sleeping on a cot, so I went to the sink by moonlight. I could see very little in the dimly-lit room, so I felt around on the countertop until I came to the little round ball, swallowed it and must have fallen asleep in a few minutes. After all, I had taken a nerve pill, hadn't I?

We got up the next morning, ate breakfast, and went back upstairs to pack and get ready to go home. But what was this? A little white pill, laying on the counter by the sink. Looking around a little more, I saw other little round things too. Bits and crumbs of food and several ladybugs crawling around the screen. I'll let you guess what finally helped me sleep.

Finally, a bit of Amish wisdom about dealing with worldly things:

- Happiness involves not letting the things we can't have, don't have, and shouldn't have spoil our enjoyment of the things we can and do have. A lesson is learning to be happy without the things we cannot or ought not have.

- Old timers can recall when a fellow wondered where his next dollar was coming from, instead of where it had gone.

- The way to live with no money is to stay out of town, stay home, and make do with what is there.

- *Recipe for Happiness*

  2 heaping cups of patience
  2 hearts full of love
  1 dash of laughter
  2 hands full of generosity
  1 head full of understanding
  1 tbsp. courtesy

  Mix well with humility. Sprinkle generously with kindness and plenty of faith. Spread over a lifetime. Serve to family, friends, and strangers.

Well, I have now really come to the end, and leave you with one last verse:

## GET UP AND GO

*Well folks, I've had it, but I ain't got it now.*
*The old git up and go has left me somehow.*
*Oh, I get a notion, but just now and then,*
*That I'm still just as good as I was way back when.*
*But I may as well face it for I know it ain't so,*
*For it takes all I got just to get up and go.*

\* \* \* \* \*

Thank you for staying with me through these pages. I hope that some of what I've shared from my experiences will be useful to you, and if so, I give credit to God who has blessed me during my growing years, while raising my family, and now during my golden years. May God bless you also.

# APPENDIX -

# SOURCES FOR THE RESOURCES

**Mail Order Herb Suppliers:**

- **Chupp's Herbs and Fabrics**, 27539-GAP Londick, Burr Oak, MI 49030. (7 1/2 miles N. of Sturgis on M-66, 1/2 miles west on Londick.) They have prompt U.P.S. delivery in the U.S. and Canada, and a free catalog, but appreciate it if you send four stamps for postage.

- **Indiana Botanic Gardens**, P.O. Box 5, Hammond, IN 46325

**Books**

- If you are interested in making homemade soap, maybe you can find Ann Branson's book, *Soap - Making and Enjoying It*, published in 1975 by Workman Publishing, Co., NY.

- Two herbals I refer to are:

  Henrietta A. Diers-Rau, *Healing with Herbs--Nature's Way to Better Health*, Arco Publishing, 219 Park Ave. S., NY, NY 10003, published in

1980. This may be out of print now, but could possibly be available through used book shops,

Clarence Meyer, *American Folk Medicine*, New American Library, New York, published in 1973. This is available through Indiana Botanic Gardens for $10.96 (Order # POOFOLK).

## Newspapers

The Amish advertize to one another in our national newspaper, *The Budget*, Sugar Creek Budget Publishing Co, Inc., P.O. Box 249, Sugar Creek, OH 44681-0249 (216) 852-4634), and also in *Die Botschaft*, published by Brookshire Publications, Inc., 200 Hazel St, Lancaster, PA 17604. Write to them about subscriptions.

# INDEX

*P*lain and Happy Living makes an excellent gift
   for any occasion. Share Emma Byler's wisdom
and hints with your family and friends, as so many
others have already done. Buy several copies to
have on hand for when you wish to give a unique,
thought-provoking keepsake.

Single copy price $10.95; 3 or more $9.95 each. (Ohio
residents, add 7% sales tax). Add $3.50 for the first book
and $1.00 for each additional book for shipping and order
processing.

Wholesale prices are also available. Write us on your
organization's letterhead and include your sales tax I.D.
number.

– – – – – – – – – – – – – – – CLIP AND MAIL ORDER FORM – – – – – – – – – – –

Please send me _____ copy(ies) of *Plain and Happy Living: Amish
Recipes and Remedies*.  Enclosed is my check or money order, payable
to Goosefoot Acres Press, in the amount of $_____.

☐ Please send the book(s) I've ordered and add me to your mailing
list to hear about other Goosefoot Acres books and services.

☐ I don't want to order now, but please add my name to your
mailing list.

Name: _____

Address: _____

_____

Telephone: _____

Mail this form and your check to:

**Goosefoot Acres Press**
*Division of Goosefoot Acres, Inc.*
P.O. Box 18016
Cleveland, OH  44118-0016
(216) 932-2145